Internal Assessment for Psychology

Skills for success

For the IB Diploma

Jean-Marc Lawton

The Publishers would like to thank the following for permission to reproduce copyright material.

Photo credit

p.28 © Gordon Willard Allport.

Author's acknowledgement

For Rob Parrish, who resides in Valhalla.

Every effort has been made to trace all copyright holders, but if any have been inadvertently overlooked, the Publishers will be pleased to make the necessary arrangements at the first opportunity.

Although every effort has been made to ensure that website addresses are correct at time of going to press, Hodder Education cannot be held responsible for the content of any website mentioned in this book. It is sometimes possible to find a relocated web page by typing in the address of the home page for a website in the URL window of your browser.

Hachette UK's policy is to use papers that are natural, renewable and recyclable products and made from wood grown in well-managed forests and other controlled sources. The logging and manufacturing processes are expected to conform to the environmental regulations of the country of origin.

Orders: please contact Hachette UK Distribution, Hely Hutchinson Centre, Milton Road, Didcot, Oxfordshire, OX11 7HH. Telephone: +44 (0)1235 827827. Email education@hachette.co.uk Lines are open from 9 a.m. to 5 p.m., Monday to Friday. You can also order through our website: www.hoddereducation.co.uk

ISBN: 978 1510 449527

© Jean-Marc Lawton 2018

First published in 2018 by

Hodder Education,

An Hachette UK Company

Carmelite House

50 Victoria Embankment

London EC4Y 0DZ

www.hoddereducation.com

Impression number   10 9 8 7 6 5 4 3

Year   2022

All rights reserved. Apart from any use permitted under UK copyright law, no part of this publication may be reproduced or transmitted in any form or by any means, electronic or mechanical, including photocopying and recording, or held within any information storage and retrieval system, without permission in writing from the publisher or under licence from the Copyright Licensing Agency Limited. Further details of such licences (for reprographic reproduction) may be obtained from the Copyright Licensing Agency Limited, www.cla.co.uk

Cover photo © nosha – stock.adobe.com

Illustrations by Aptara Inc.

Typeset in GoudyStd 10/12 pts by Aptara Inc.

Printed and bound by CPI Group (UK) Ltd, Croydon CR0 4YY

A catalogue record for this title is available from the British Library.

Contents

Introduction		iv
Section 1	**IB Psychology and the internal assessment**	2
Chapter 1	What is the internal assessment?	4
Chapter 2	The assessment of the experimental study	8
Section 2	**Experimental skills and abilities**	10
Chapter 3	Research methods	12
Chapter 4	Mini-practicals	20
Chapter 5	Descriptive and inferential statistical analysis	37
Section 3	**Carrying out the internal assessment**	54
Chapter 6	Planning your experimental study	56
Chapter 7	Conducting the study	63
Chapter 8	Writing the research report	64
'Tick-list' for conducting an experimental study		76
Template for mini-practicals		78
References		83
Index		84

Introduction

Psychology can be defined as *the scientific study of mind and behaviour* (though it should be remembered that psychology also includes non-scientific elements in its subject matter and methods of investigation). In order to discover 'truths' about the mind and behaviour (which are generally expressed in the form of theories, explanations and models), psychological research has to be undertaken, with the vast majority of such research being scientific in nature and generally carried out in the form of experiments, as in other scientific subjects, such as biology, chemistry and physics.

Throughout the IB psychology course, you will learn about psychological theories, explanations, models, practical applications and so forth, which are based upon and have been assessed by research studies. Indeed, you will be required to have a knowledge of all these elements, including specific research studies, as questions may be asked about them in your final examination papers. You will also need a knowledge of the methods that underpin the means by which research is carried out. This includes their evaluation in terms of strengths and limitations, as again these elements can have questions asked about them in your final examination papers.

You will also learn, especially when writing essays (which will form part of your final examination papers), that evaluation is often centred on what specific research studies suggest about the **validity** (accuracy) of theories, explanations and models. You will consider the effectiveness of practical applications, as well as methodological criticisms of studies themselves in terms of how their strengths and limitations might affect the validity of conclusions drawn.

> **Key definition**
> **Validity** – the extent to which results accurately measure what they are supposed to measure.

You will receive formal tuition from your teachers about these required elements, but a more effective way to learn about them is to actually conduct some research yourself. In essence, as well as learning about psychology from your teachers, learning how to be a psychologist from practical experience is essential to understanding the subject.

To allow you to develop and apply these skills and knowledge, the internal assessment is an integral part of the overall qualification for psychology.

■ The internal assessment

The internal assessment is a compulsory part of the IB psychology course. Aside from studying core and optional topics for which you will sit formal examinations at the end of the course, you are also required to investigate a published psychological study, theory or model, by planning, carrying out and writing up a practical investigation in the form of an experimental study of your own.

The general idea behind the internal assessment is to allow you to demonstrate that you can apply, in a practical way, the psychological skills and knowledge you have learned during your studying of the subject, but with more freedom to do so than is possible in an examination setting. The internal assessment can be conducted much more liberally, as there are far fewer time limitations and other constraints than occur when sitting an examination. You also have the freedom to conduct a practical investigation of your own choosing, giving you the opportunity to explore an area of psychology that you personally find interesting and motivating.

The internal assessment will generally be undertaken throughout the course and not treated as a separate activity conducted when all the teaching of topics has finished. There is a degree of teaching that needs to take place, though, before you can realistically set out to undertake your practical investigation. This especially concerns the research methods module of the course, during which you will learn not just about why research is carried out in psychology, but also how it is carried out in its many different forms, and what the strengths and weaknesses of different research methods are. Without a knowledge of research methods, you will not fully understand the purpose of carrying out a practical investigation in psychology. More importantly, you will not be able to design the individual components required for your experimental study.

You will also need to be fully aware of what data is and how and why it is analysed in the descriptive and inferential ways that it is within psychology. Again, you will learn this during the research methods module of the course.

You will probably also have studied some other topics, too, before embarking on the internal assessment, as by studying some topic areas you will begin to understand how psychology works, in terms of how research that psychologists carry out underpins the theories, models and explanations that make up the subject, and the practical applications that are based on this knowledge. The studying of topic areas will also provide some feeling for which area of psychology you might wish to base your experimental study upon.

Ultimately, it will be teachers of the IB psychology course who will decide what order to teach topics in, and indeed which particular optional topics to teach to their students. It will also be teachers of the subject who decide when their students should undertake the internal assessment, how this will occur and what time frame they will have to complete the work in. However, the main responsibility for this important piece of work belongs to individual students and so you should be aware from the start what it involves and what you will have to do (and when). You should also start to form some idea of what specific psychological area, in terms of the actual investigation, you might wish to perform research in. All potential ideas for the practical investigation should be discussed with teachers, as they will be able to advise whether they are acceptable from an ethical point of view (especially due to the sensitive nature of many topic areas in psychology), as well as whether they are feasible and practical to actually carry out.

Section 1 IB Psychology

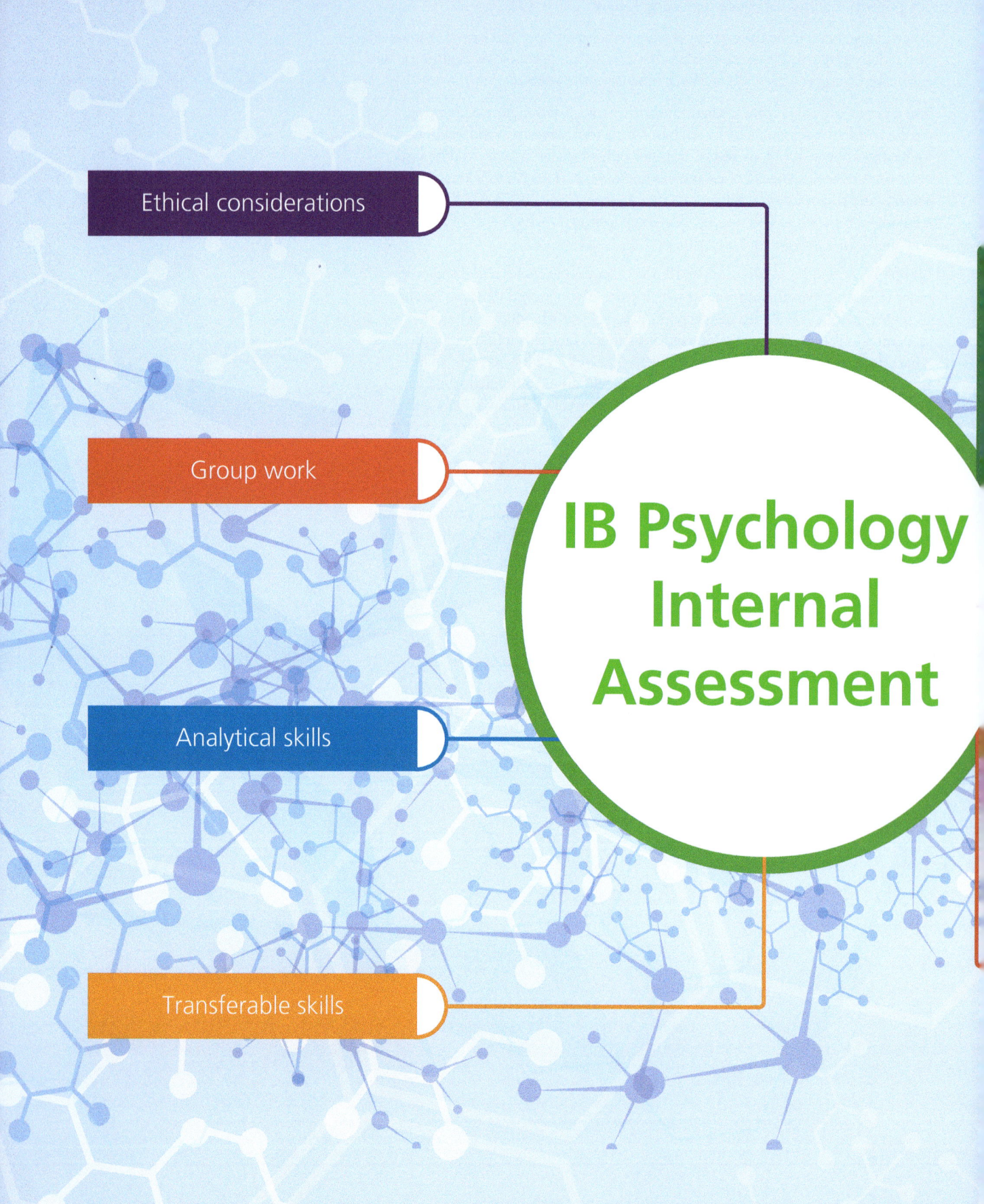

and the internal assessment

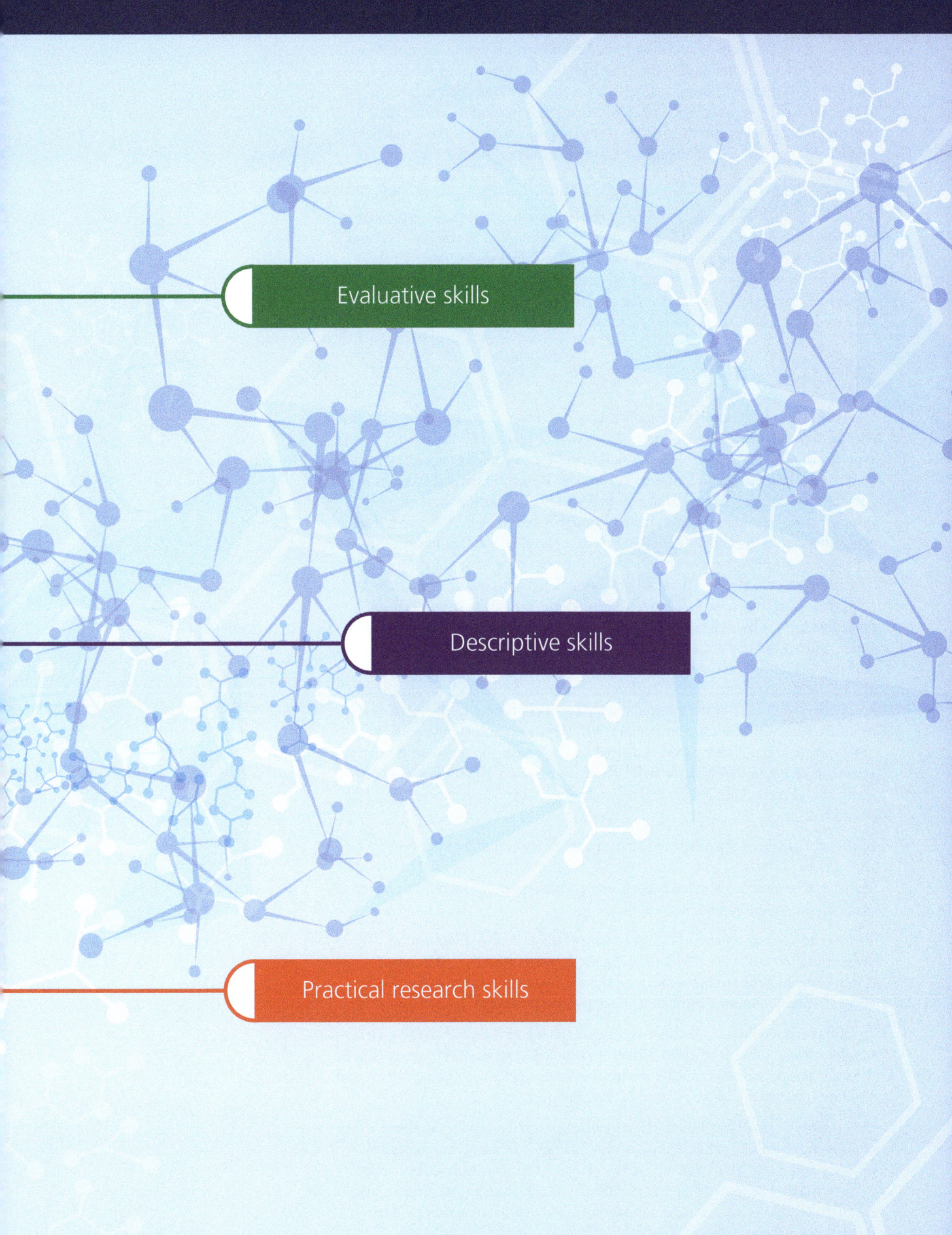

1 What is the internal assessment?

At the end of your course you will sit formal examinations, with your completed exam papers formally marked by specialist examiners appointed by the IB. This is a process called external assessment, as the marking occurs externally to your school. However, the practical investigation is marked in a different way through a process known as internal assessment. Each individual student's teacher will monitor the conducting of their experimental study (to ensure it is done in accordance with the guidelines set out by the IB) and then will mark their practical investigation (according to a set of criteria and mark allocations set out by the IB). The marks awarded by the teacher are then checked through a process known as moderation, where specialists appointed by the board review the work undertaken and its internal assessment. So, in a sense, although the experimental study is marked by internal assessment, this does also involve an element of external assessment, via the moderation process, to ensure that the work undertaken is assessed fairly and reliably.

Skills

The main skills involved in the conducting of the internal assessment are *practical research skills*, which concern a knowledge of how to plan and carry out an experimental study successfully. Such skills can be studied, for example, by reading (and completing the assessment exercises in) the 'Research methods' section in Chapter four of your textbook (Lawton & Willard, 2018). However, these skills can only truly be understood and honed through actual usage. This comes from experience and it may be the case that your teacher gives you familiarity of them through organizing some mini-practicals during class time. If not, and even if so, there is no reason why individual or small groups of students cannot have a go in their own time at replicating (repeating) some famous studies, albeit in a simplified form. This will help you get a feel for the organizational skills required and to learn some of the dos and don'ts of conducting research, which will be of benefit when conducting the actual experimental study. Some suggestions for and guidance on how to conduct such mini-practicals (to be undertaken before conducting the study for the internal assessment) occurs later in this book (see page 20). Although there are no formal marks for the planning and conducting of the practical (marks are awarded instead for the writing up of the report of the investigation), your investigation will be more successful if the study is carefully planned and carried out, which will only occur with a good execution of practical research skills.

In the writing up of the report of the study, there is a requirement for appropriate knowledge to be expressed. *Descriptive skills* are required for this and marks will be awarded for clearly outlining each element of the procedure, for example the sampling technique used.

There is also a requirement in the writing up of the practical investigation for appraisal, so *evaluative skills* will be required. Marks are awarded in terms of exploration of the strengths and weaknesses of your research, for example strengths and limitations of the design, sample and procedure.

An additional requirement in the writing up of the report is that of analysis, for which *analytical skills* are required. Marks are awarded in terms of how the data from the study is processed and conclusions are met, for example through appropriate and accurate application of descriptive and inferential statistics.

One last type of skill involved in the conducting of the internal assessment is that of *transferable skills*, which concern abilities that are relevant and useful across different situations. Skills that are learned in other sciences, such as those relevant to experimental design, will be transferable to the carrying out of psychological research (and skills learned carrying out the experimental study may well be transferable to other science subjects).

Type of skill	Description of skill
Practical research skills	Skills associated with the planning and carrying out of psychological studies
Descriptive skills	Skills associated with the outlining of relevant knowledge
Evaluative skills	Skills associated with appraisal of research methods and conclusions drawn
Analytical skills	Skills associated with the processing of data to draw valid conclusions
Transferable skills	Skills that are portable between different academic disciplines

Table 1.1 Summary of skills involved in the conducting of the internal assessment

IB requirements

SL/HL requirements

The requirements for SL and HL students in doing the internal assessment are exactly the same; that is to investigate a published study, theory or model relevant to their learning in psychology, by carrying out an experimental study and then reporting the findings.

SL students

For SL students, the internal assessment will comprise 25% of the overall marks. The marks will be assessed and awarded in relation to the quality of the research report submitted.

HL students

For HL students, the internal assessment will comprise 20% of the overall marks. The marks will be assessed and awarded in relation to the quality of the research report submitted.

Specific requirements of the IB for the experimental study

Seeking advice from teachers

- You should seek advice from your teachers on:

    1 The requirements of the IB for the internal assessment
    2 What experiment to choose
    3 What practical and ethical issues need to be considered
    4 How your work will be assessed in terms of the assessment criteria.

- You can (and should) discuss your internal assessment work with your teacher and should not be penalized (in terms of marks awarded) for doing so.

- A teacher is allowed to give verbal and written advice on how the research report of the study could be improved for ONE draft (practice) version of the study. The second version submitted to the teacher has to be the final version and cannot be changed once it has been submitted.

Working in groups

- When planning and carrying out the study, you will be required to work in groups of between two and four students.
- SL and HL students are allowed to work together as members of a group in the planning and carrying out of their experimental study.
- Groups can include virtual (online) members, who are studying IB psychology at another school.
- Groups can also include students studying other related courses, either IB or non-IB.

- Because the planning and carrying out of the experimental study is done by a group of students, the research method, materials, participants and operationalization of the independent and dependent variables will be the same for these students and will result from the group working together.
- Once a study has been carried out and data collected, group members cannot work together anymore – this includes the analysis of the data, conclusions drawn and the evaluation of the study within the research report. Indeed, group members should not even discuss the results of the study once the data has been collected and each group member has a copy.

Choosing an experiment

- The topic chosen to base the experimental study on can be taken from any area of psychology (not just those on the specification).
- The theory, model or study on which the experimental study is based must have appeared in a peer-reviewed journal.
- The connection between the theory, model or study on which your experimental study is based must be linked to your aims and objectives, and the reason for conducting the experiment should be explained.

Other specific requirements

- When the experimental study has been carried out and data collected, each student in a group must work independently of each other (by themselves) in writing up the research report, including the analysis of data, the conclusions drawn and evaluative points made.
- The same piece of work cannot be submitted to meet the requirements of the internal assessment and the extended essay.
- The research study cannot be of any other method than that of an experiment.
- Your work must be completely your own with no plagiarism occurring (presenting the work of another as your own). Referencing others' work (such as by describing previous relevant research) is allowable, as long as sources are credited.
- Ethical considerations must be adhered to in planning, carrying out and writing up the report.

Dos and don'ts for the internal assessment

- You are only allowed to have one **independent variable (IV)** in your experimental study.
- The research study on which your experiment is based may have several conditions for the IV. Therefore, you can either replicate all the conditions (repeat them exactly by having all the original conditions of the IV in your study), or simplify the experiment so that there are only two conditions of the IV).
- The way in which the IV is **operationalized** (defined) may differ from the original research study, in order to suit the specific circumstances of each student's experimental study.
- Independent variables that are based on pre-existing characteristics of participants are not acceptable for the internal assessment. These include:
    1. *Gender* (comparing the performance of males and females)
    2. *Age* (comparing participants of different age groups)
    3. *Native language* (comparing speakers of two different languages)
    4. *Culture* (comparing participants from different cultural groups)
    5. *Education* (comparing participants from different classes/schools)
    6. *Socio-economic status* (comparing participants of different wealth or class groupings)
    7. *Handedness* (comparing left- and right-handed participants).

> **Key definitions**
>
> **Independent variable** – the factor manipulated by researchers in an investigation.
>
> **Operationalization of variables** – the process of defining variables into measurable factors.
>
> **Placebos** – harmless substances given to participants that they are told will have some specific effect.
>
> **Ingestion and exhalation** – studies involving eating, drinking, smoking, taking drugs, etc.
>
> **Deprivation** – studies involving denial of essential requirements, such as sleep, food, etc.

> **Expert tip**
>
> In essence, this means that a quasi-experimental design would not be permissible (see page 17).
>
> Also not acceptable are experiments that include:
>
> 1. **Placebos**
> 2. **Ingestion and exhalation**
> 3. **Deprivation** – this would include not just studies of humans, but animals too, as deprivation would lower an animal's fitness, which is an ethical consideration of research performed upon animals.

■ Ethical guidelines

The planning, undertaking and writing up of the experimental study must all be done in terms of ethical guidelines set out by the IB.

- No experiments are permitted that cause stress, anxiety, pain or discomfort.
- No experiments involving deception or any forms of harm are permitted.
- Experiments should be appropriate to the sensitivities of specific schools, communities and cultures that they are being conducted in.
- Experiments involving unjustified deception, involuntary participation (see 'Field experiments', page 16) or invasion of privacy (including subjecting participants to inappropriate use of information, images, emails, communication technology and the internet) are to be avoided – there may be rare occasions when such infringements cannot be avoided, but the approval to do so should be gained from other experienced psychologists before proceeding.
- Partial deception, in terms of not fully informing participants in advance about the requirements/purpose of a study, because this would strongly affect the behaviour of participants and thus invalidate findings, are permissible if such studies incur no harm and participants are fully debriefed at the end and have the right to withdraw their data at this point. However, conformity and obedience studies that involve such partial deception are not permissible.
- Consent to participate must be gained by participants signing a consent form. Implied consent is not permissible.
- Participants should be informed of the aims and objectives of the experiment.
- Participants should be given the right to withdraw at any time from the study before the study begins. Pressure must not be put on participants to continue if they choose to withdraw.
- Children under the age of 12 cannot be used as they cannot give informed consent. Children between the ages of 12 and 16 can participate if fully informed consent is gained from their parents or guardians. If an experiment is conducted with children in a school, the written consent of teachers must also be gained.
- Informed consent cannot be gained from anyone who is not in a fit state of mind or who cannot respond freely and independently.
- Participants should be fully debriefed about the purposes of a study at the finish, with the right to withdraw again given.
- Anonymity should be assured for all participants, including after the study has finished.
- Participants should be shown the results of the study and have any deception explained to them.
- An experiment should be stopped immediately if any participant shows signs of distress.
- Non-human animal studies are not permitted.
- All data should only be used for purposes agreed to by participants, kept confidential and not be disclosed to others.
- You should monitor the way in which your peers conduct research. For instance, you should ensure your peers work in ethically acceptable ways.
- Experimental studies conducted online are subject to the same ethical considerations, and data collected online should be deleted once the research is complete.

2 The assessment of the experimental study

Assessment criteria

How research reports are marked

The IB has *assessment criteria* against which research reports will be judged, initially internally by a teacher and later on externally by a moderator appointed by the board. Therefore, each section of the report should be written in a way that attempts to maximize attainment of the marks available for each assessment criterion.

Each of the assessment criteria has a *level descriptor* that describes what needs to be achieved for that particular level of the criterion. The levels within the assessment criteria each have their own range of marks.

Teachers will assess their students' work through awarding marks with reference to the assessment criteria levels. External moderators appointed by the IB will check the marks awarded with reference to the same assessment criteria levels in the same way.

The same assessment criteria and levels are used for the work of both SL and HL students.

As the IB recommend that the assessment criteria are made available to students, they will now be outlined and explained.

Introduction component (6 marks)

Marks are awarded in this component for an explanation of the theory/model upon which the experimental study is based, with the aims and hypotheses (including the IV and DV) of the study linked to the theory/model.

Marks	Level descriptor
5–6	• The aim of the investigation is stated and its relevance explained.
	• The theory or model upon which the student's investigation is based is described and the link to the student's investigation is explained.
	• The independent and dependent variables are stated and operationalized in the null or experimental (research) hypotheses.
3–4	• The aim of the investigation is stated and its relevance is identified but not explained.
	• The theory or model upon which the student's investigation is based is described but the link to the student's investigation is not explained.
	• The independent and dependent variables are correctly stated in the null or experimental (research) hypotheses, but are not operationalized.
1–2	• The aim of the investigation is stated but its relevance is not identified.
	• The theory or model upon which the student's investigation is based is identified but the description is incomplete or contains errors.
	• Null and/or experimental (research) hypotheses are stated, but do not correctly identify the independent or dependent variables.
0	• The work does not reach the standard described by the descriptors above.

Table 2.1 Level descriptors for the introduction component

Exploration component (4 marks)

As the exploration component takes place during the group collaboration phase of the study (though not the reporting of it), there are relatively fewer marks available for this component than others.

Marks are awarded in this component for an explanation of the methodology and design used in the experimental study.

Marks	Level descriptor
3–4	- The research design is explained. - The sampling technique is explained. - The choice of participants is explained. - Controlled variables are explained. - The choice of materials is explained.
1–2	- The research design is described. - The sampling technique is described. - Characteristics of the participants are described. - Controlled variables are described. - The materials used are described.
0	- The work does not reach the standard described by the descriptors above.

Table 2.2 Level descriptors for the exploration component

Analysis component (6 marks)

Marks are awarded in this component for appropriate selection and correct application of descriptive and inferential statistical techniques, with interpretations of the data accurately linked to the hypotheses.

Marks	Level descriptor
5–6	- Descriptive and inferential statistics are appropriately and accurately applied. - The graph is correctly presented and addresses the hypothesis. - The statistical findings are interpreted with regard to the data and are linked to the hypothesis.
3–4	- Appropriate descriptive and inferential statistics are applied but there are errors. - The graph addresses the hypothesis but contains errors. - The statistical findings are stated but either not interpreted with regard to the data or not linked to the hypothesis.
1–2	- Only descriptive or inferential statistics are applied. - A correct graphing technique is chosen but the graph does not address the hypothesis. - There is no clear statement of findings.
0	- The work does not reach the standard described by the descriptors above.

Table 2.3 Level descriptors for the analysis component

Evaluation component (6 marks)

Marks in this component are awarded for discussion of findings in relation to the background theory/model, strengths and limitations of the methodology and design used, with suggested modifications linked to the reported strengths and limitations and fully justified.

Marks	Level descriptor
5–6	- The findings of the student's investigation are discussed with reference to the background theory or model. - Strengths and limitations of the design, sample and procedure are stated and explained and are relevant to the investigation. - Modifications are explicitly linked to the limitations of the student's investigation and are fully justified.
3–4	- The findings of the student's investigation are described with reference to the background theory or model. - Strengths and limitations of the design, sample or procedure are stated and described and are relevant to the investigation. - Modifications are described but not explicitly linked to the limitations of the student's investigation.
1–2	- The findings of the student's investigation are described without reference to the background theory or model. - Strengths and limitations of the design, sample or procedure are stated but are not directly relevant to the hypothesis. - One or more modifications are stated.
0	- The work does not reach the standard described by the descriptors above.

Table 2.4 Level descriptors for the evaluation component

Section 2 Experimental skills

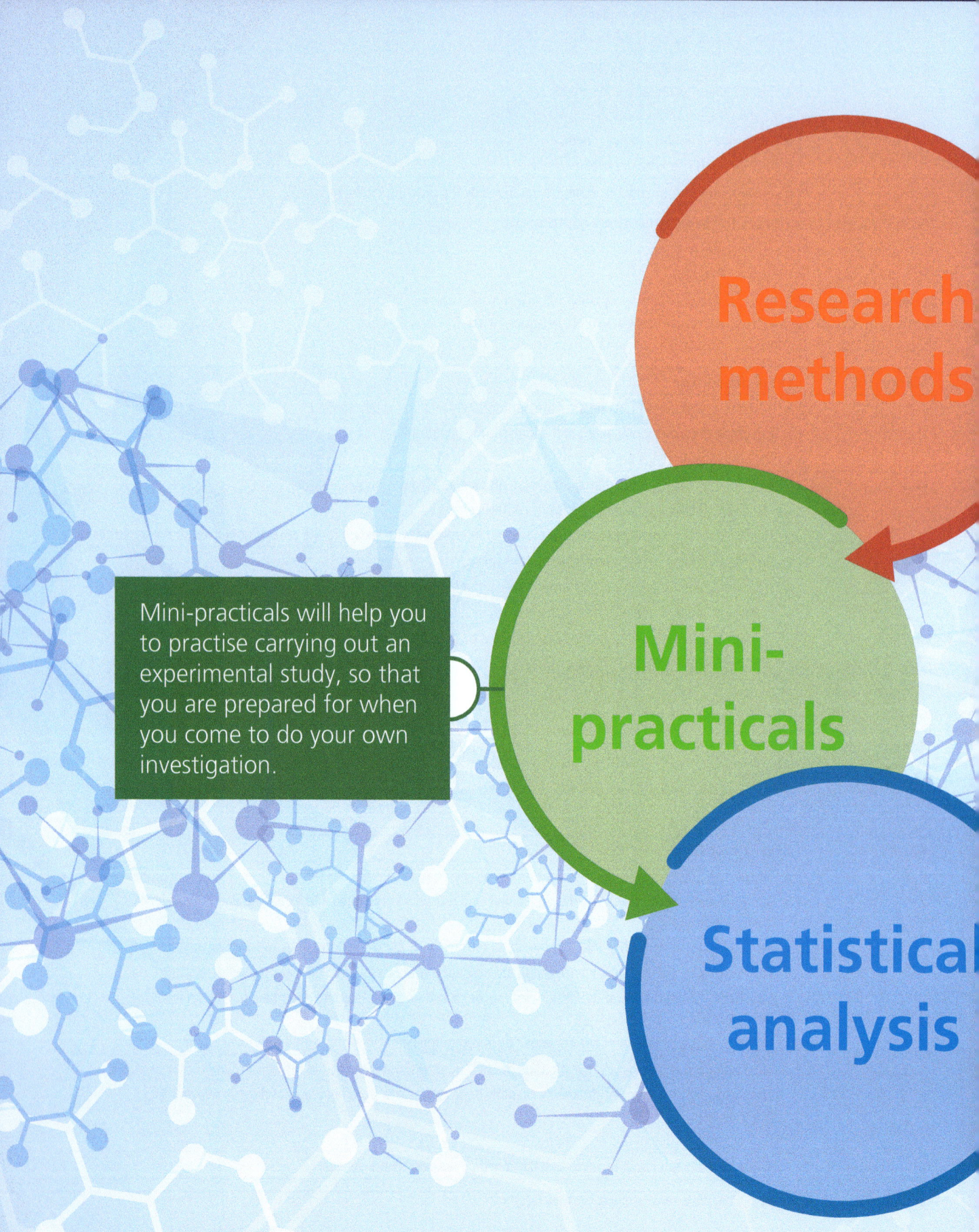

Mini-practicals will help you to practise carrying out an experimental study, so that you are prepared for when you come to do your own investigation.

and abilities

Research is the foundation of psychology, and an understanding of research methods will help you to plan your internal assessment investigation.

You will need to analyse the data using descriptive statistical analysis (describing the data in numerical form) and inferential statistical analysis (using your data to find patterns of generalizations).

3 Research methods

This section covers the important considerations in terms of elements of research methods that will need to be understood and utilized in the effective planning and carrying out of the experimental study for the internal assessment.

Reference to these relevant elements of research will help you make important decisions in the planning and carrying out of your study.

Research is the foundation of psychology; it is what allows the construction of theories, explanations and models. It is also what assesses how valid such theories, explanations and models are, and how effective the practical applications are that are based upon them.

There are various research methods, both scientific and non-scientific, each with its limitations and strengths and each more applicable to different circumstances. However, we shall limit ourselves here to an exploration of the experimental research method, as that is the only one permissible for the internal assessment.

The experimental method

The experimental method is a scientific research method that involves the manipulation of variables to determine **causality** (cause and effect relationships). A variable is anything that can occur differently in some way in an experiment and thus has an effect on the findings.

Participants are randomly allocated (without bias in selection) to the different conditions (testing groups), which means that the conditions should be fairly equal in terms of the types of people in the testing groups.

> **Key definitions**
> **Causality** – cause and effect relationships.
> **Dependent variable (DV)** – the factor measured by researchers in an investigation.

Independent and dependent variables

All procedures in an experiment (everything that occurs) should be *standardized* (kept the same for all participants). The intention of this is that all variables in an experiment are *controlled* (kept the same for all participants), so that the effect of the one variable being tested, the *independent variable* (IV), can be clearly seen and recorded.

So, in your experimental study you will require an IV, which will need to be clearly *operationalized* (defined) so it can be manipulated (changed) between your experimental conditions (testing groups). It gets its name from the fact that it is independent of the participants' control, as it is manipulated instead by the researcher.

The IV is manipulated to see its effect on a **dependent variable (DV)**, which is operationalized as a measurement of some kind. In your experimental study, your DV will be a measurement of the effect of your IV upon the different experimental conditions.

So, for example, if you wished to see the effect of sleep upon reaction time, you could have two experimental conditions (which participants had been randomly allocated to): one where participants had no sleep last night and one where participants had, say, eight hours' sleep last night. The IV would be sleep or no sleep, as this is the one variable that alters between the two conditions and is manipulated by researchers (as they decide, by random selection, who is in each testing group). The DV could be how long it took to press a button when a light came on, in other words a measurement of time.

Extraneous and confounding variables

In order to see clearly the effect of the IV upon the DV, all other variables in an experiment should be controlled so that they don't vary in any of the experimental conditions or between participants; in other words, they should remain constant for all testing groups. In your experiment, **extraneous variables** will be any variables, other than the IV, which could have an effect on the DV. You will need to control these in order to establish *causality* (cause and effect relationships). If something else other than the IV has affected your DV, you will not be able to state that it was the IV that caused the effect upon the DV.

Uncontrolled extraneous variables can become **confounding variables** which confound (confuse) the results by affecting the DV. In effect, extraneous variables could affect the DV (and thus your results) and so need to be controlled, while confounding variables are extraneous variables that were not controlled and did affect the DV.

In the example given of testing the effect of sleep upon reaction times, whether participants had eaten breakfast could be an extraneous variable, as having or not having breakfast might affect participants' reaction times in pressing a button when a light came on. Therefore, you would need to ensure all participants in both conditions had breakfast (or not) so that it did not affect the DV. If you did not control this, it might become a confounding variable and not allow you to see the effect of sleep upon reaction times. You will need to consider what things could be extraneous variables in your experiment and decide in advance how you would control them.

There are three main types of extraneous variables you will have to control:

1 *Participant variables* – these are variables concerned with participants themselves. For example, participants' age, gender, level of intelligence and so on. If you had everybody in one condition who was over 40 years of age and everyone in the other condition who was under 20, then this factor could have a confounding effect upon the DV (reaction times). To control it, you would need to ensure that there was a balance of types of participants within your testing groups.

2 *Situational variables* – these are variables that concern the experimental setting (the testing environment). For example, temperature, noise levels and so on. If one testing group performed the study in a hotter or noisier environment than the other testing group, then that might affect their reaction times in pressing a button when a light came on, rather than the effect of having had eight hours' sleep or not. Therefore, these factors would need to be controlled by making sure the environmental conditions under which your experiment takes place are the same for all participants.

3 *Experimenter variables* – these are variables concerning changes in the personality, appearance and behaviour of researchers. For example, a researcher who is laid-back and friendly with some participants and stricter and more formal with others might have an effect on their reaction times. Therefore, it is important that the same researcher tests all participants and acts in the same way with all participants to ensure it is the IV only that affects the DV.

> **Key definitions**
>
> **Extraneous variables** – variables other than the IV that might affect the DV.
>
> **Confounding variables** – uncontrolled extraneous variables that negatively affect results.
>
> **Demand characteristics** – a research effect where participants form impressions of the research purpose and unconsciously alter their behaviour accordingly.

Demand characteristics

Aside from extraneous and confounding variables, when you conduct your experimental study there is also the risk of **demand characteristics** not allowing you to establish causality by clearly seeing the effect of the IV on the DV. Demand characteristics involve interactions between participants and researchers that affect participants' behaviour so that they do not behave as they naturally would.

There are generally four ways in which demand characteristics might affect participant behaviour so that results are confounded:

1 Believing that they have worked out the purpose of the study and so acting in an unnatural way that they believe the researcher wants them to do in order to 'prove' their hypothesis.

2. Believing that they have worked out the purpose of the study and so acting in an unnatural manner in order to 'mess up' the study and produce results that will 'disprove' the hypothesis. This is known as the *'screw you phenomenon'*.

3. Knowing that they are taking part in a study and so acting in an unnatural manner out of nervousness or fear of evaluation.

4. Knowing that they are taking part in a study and so acting in an unnatural manner due to *social desirability bias*, where participants behave in a manner that they believe society would expect of them (such as by not expressing racist beliefs even if they hold such views).

A method that you can use to minimize the risk of demand characteristics (which would be reported in the methodology section of your practical report) is the *single-blind procedure*. This involves participants having no idea which condition of a study they are in. For example, in clinical trials of drugs for use with mental disorders, participants often do not know if they are in a condition which involves taking a drug, or in a condition that involves taking a placebo (dummy drug). However, this technique is not always possible to use. For instance, in the example of an experiment investigating whether sleep affects reaction times, participants would know whether or not they slept last night.

Use of an independent groups design (see page 17) can help reduce the chances of demand characteristics, as each participant only does one condition of the study and so has less chance to form an opinion of what the purpose of the study is and adjust their behaviour to try to 'prove' or 'disprove' what they believe to be the hypothesis.

Investigator effects

Investigator effects are the ways in which researchers unconsciously influence the results of research and can occur in three main ways:

1. *Physical characteristics* – physical aspects of researchers can affect participants' behaviour. For example, participants may try to impress researchers of one gender more than another.

2. *Personal characteristics* – personal aspects of researchers can affect participants' behaviour, like their accent or tone of voice. For example, a participant may behave differently to a researcher with a posh voice than to someone with a more regional accent.

3. *Researcher bias* – researchers may be unconsciously biased to interpreting participants' behaviour in such a way as to support their hypothesis. In other words, they find what they want to find or expect to find. For example, researchers may unknowingly phrase questions in a way that suggests to participants how they would like them to answer.

A method that you can use to minimize the risk of investigator effects (which would be reported in the methodology section of your practical report) is the *double-blind procedure*, where neither the participants nor the researchers know what conditions participants are in. This prevents researchers 'feeding' clues to the participants as to which condition they are in and thus how they would like them to behave (which therefore reduces the chances of demand characteristics). For example, in clinical drug trials, neither the researchers nor the participants would know who was taking the drug being tested or a placebo. Again, though, this technique is not always practically possible to use.

Types of experiments

There are four basic types of experiments, though as not all of them strictly follow the experimental design (see page 17), some are not considered to be 'full' types by psychologists.

The IB has set out requirements that generally exclude certain types of experiment being carried out as part of the internal assessment for the psychology qualification.

Laboratory experiments

Laboratory experiments are performed in a controlled environment (a laboratory) using a standardized procedure (one that is the same for all participants). Participants are randomly allocated (without bias) to the experimental conditions and an IV is manipulated (set up) by researchers. For example, Marsh et al. (1997) tested whether expecting to have to recall information affected the duration of short-term memory (STM). Participants were randomly allocated to two conditions: firstly, a condition where they were given information verbally, but not told they were going to have to recall it; and secondly, a condition where they were given the same information verbally in the same way, but were told they were going to have to recall it. All variables except the IV (whether they were told recall would occur) were controlled (kept the same) for all participants, with the DV (a measurement of the effect of the IV) being how long the information was stored within STM. Recall was possible for a significantly shorter time when participants did not expect to have to recall the information than when they did, which suggested duration of STM is affected by whether or not recall is required.

> **Expert tip**
> A simple laboratory experiment will be possible for students to perform according to the guidelines set out by the IB.

■ Strengths of laboratory experiments

- Allow a high degree of control over variables and for the IV to be fully operationalized (defined) and the DV to be clearly measured, which leads to greater accuracy and objectivity.

- Demonstrate causality (cause and effect relationships) due to strict control of variables. Therefore, any effect (a change in the value of the DV between conditions) must be due to the manipulation (altering) of the IV and no other factor.

- Can be easily replicated (repeated to check findings), as they are done under controlled conditions and with a standardized procedure, making it easy to repeat the study exactly as before.

■ Weaknesses of laboratory experiments

- There is low **external validity**, because high degrees of control make experimental situations artificial and unlike real life. Therefore, it can be difficult to generalize findings to settings beyond those of the laboratory.

- Demand characteristics exist because participants are aware they are being tested; they may, therefore, alter their behaviour and not act normally, which may confound the results.

- Experimenter bias can occur, where researchers' expectations and desires affect the interpretation of results and participants' behaviour, making findings invalid.

> **Key definition**
> **External validity** – the extent to which findings from a study can be generalized to others.

Field experiments

Field experiments occur in real-world settings rather than in a laboratory, and have an IV that is manipulated (set up by) the researcher. As many extraneous variables as possible are controlled and a standardized procedure followed. Whether it is fully possible with a field experiment to randomly allocate participants to the conditions is debatable. For example, Bickman (1974) assessed the effect of uniform upon obedience. A researcher dressed either as a milkman, a security guard or in casual clothes, and ordered people on the street to pick up litter they had not dropped. The IV was type of clothing worn and the DV how many people obeyed/disobeyed the order. Bickman found more people obeyed the security guard, which suggested wearing a uniform gives a person a sense of legitimate authority that makes people obey them. Participants, though, were not randomly allocated to the experimental conditions.

> **Expert tip**
>
> Although the IB guidelines do not prohibit students from performing a field experiment for their internal assessment, there are good reasons for not doing so. If participants are told the purpose of the study in advance (and the fact that they are taking place in an experiment), as they should be in order for deceit not to occur and for participants to be able to give their informed consent to take part, then the study would not be a field experiment, as participants' behaviour would not be 'natural' and so the study would not be taking place in a real-world setting. In essence it would be a laboratory experiment, albeit one where it would be more difficult to strictly control extraneous variables.
>
> Also, conducting studies in real-world settings can present potential problems of harm, as it can never be completely predicted as to what dangerous or upsetting events may occur. For example, students performing a study assessing how the availability of food affected ducks' feeding behaviour, threw different amounts of food (the IV) into different areas of a pond and counted the number of ducks at the different feeding sites (the DV). The feeding of the ducks in this way attracted the attention of a dog, which entered the pond and killed several ducks. Students attempting to remove the dog were then bitten by the dog and required hospital treatment.
>
> It is not possible to perform a field experiment for the internal assessment using animal participants, as this is specifically prohibited by the IB.

■ Strengths of field experiments

- There is higher external validity, as due to the real-world setting and participants not knowing they're in a study, behaviour is less artificial and thus findings are more generalizable to other settings.
- There are no demand characteristics, as participants do not know they are in an experiment and so do not behave artificially and invalidate the results.

■ Weaknesses of field experiments

- As there is less control over extraneous variables (due to the real-world setting) it is harder to see the effect of the IV on the DV and thus establish causality.
- Replication (to check the validity of the results) is more difficult as conditions, due to the real-world setting, would never be exactly the same again.
- There are ethical considerations of deceit, informed consent and a lack of the right to withdraw (due to participants not knowing they are in a study).
- Sample bias can occur, which invalidates results – because participants are not randomly allocated to testing groups, samples may not be comparable to each other.

Natural experiments

Natural experiments have an IV that *varies* naturally; the experimenter does not manipulate it (set it up) but merely records its effect on a DV. Participants are not randomly allocated to the experimental conditions. For example, Costello *et al.* (2003) was studying the mental health of Native Americans living on a reservation. During the study, unexpectedly, a casino was given permission to open on the reservation, which greatly increased the amount of money the residents had. This gave the researchers an opportunity to study the effect of increased income on mental health. The IV was whether or not the reservation residents had a low or a high amount of money, with the DV being a measure of mental health.

> **Expert tip**
>
> Due to the fact that the IB requires students to manipulate an IV for their experimental study, it would not be possible for a natural experiment to be conducted for the internal assessment.

Quasi-experiments

Quasi-experiments have an IV that *occurs* naturally; the experimenter does not manipulate it, but merely records its effect on a DV. For instance, gender, age or culture. Participants are thus not randomly allocated to the experimental conditions. For example, Herlitz *et al.* (1997) tested the effect of gender on episodic LTM by giving participants tasks requiring episodic memory. The IV was whether participants were male or female, with the DV being scores on a test of episodic LTM. It was found that females performed better, which suggested females have superior episodic LTM.

Both natural and quasi-experiments are not 'true' experiments as they do not involve manipulation of an IV by a researcher, nor do they involve random allocation of participants to the testing groups to reduce sample bias. Natural and quasi-experiments generally are used when it would be unethical or impractical to manipulate an IV.

> **Expert tip**
>
> IB guidelines explicitly prohibit the use of an IV for the internal assessment that is based upon pre-existing characteristics of the participants, such as gender, age, culture, etc. Therefore, and also as the internal assessment requires manipulation of an IV (which does not occur in quasi-experiments), it would not be possible for students to perform a quasi-experiment as their experimental study.
>
> This means, effectively, that the experimental study for the internal assessment should be a laboratory experiment.

Experimental design

There are three main types of experimental design: the **independent groups design (IGD)**, the **repeated measures design (RMD)** and the **matched participants design (MPD)**. There are strengths and weaknesses to each of them.

A choice must be made as to which experimental design you will use in your study, but generally the choice will be between an IGD or an RMD. The RMD is often seen as preferable to use, for reasons that will be explained, with the IGD being used when it is not advisable or possible to use an RMD. An MPD would probably present practical problems for students doing the internal assessment in being able to pre-test participants on important variables and in finding enough participants to form sufficient matching pairs.

> **Key definitions**
>
> **Independent groups design (IGD)** – experimental design in which each participant performs one condition of an experiment.
>
> **Repeated measures design (RMD)** – experimental design where each participant performs all conditions of an experiment.
>
> **Matched participants design (MPD)** – experimental design where participants are in similar pairs, with one of each pair performing each condition.

Independent groups design

An IGD uses different participants in each of the experimental conditions, so that each participant only does one condition of the experiment. In essence, different participants are tested against each other. For example, Asch's (1956) conformity study used an IGD. Half the participants had to, with no one else present, judge which of three comparison lines matched a stimulus line, while half the participants did the same task but in the presence of a number of pseudo-participants who often gave deliberately wrong answers to try and influence the real participant. There was a 32% overall conformity rate to wrong answers, which suggests that people will agree to obviously wrong answers in order to be accepted by a group.

■ Strengths of the IGD

- **No order effects** – as different participants do each condition there are no *order effects*, where the order in which conditions are done may affect the findings.
- **Less chance of demand characteristics** – as participants only do one condition each, there is less chance they can think they have worked out the purpose of the study and alter their behaviour accordingly.

> **Key definition**
> **Order effects** – where the order of presentation affects performance and so acts as an extraneous variable.

■ Weaknesses of the IGD

- **Group differences** – differences in results between the conditions may be due to *participant variables* (individual differences between participants), rather than the effect of the IV on the DV. For example, participants in one condition may be more intelligent than the other condition. Random allocation of participants to the testing conditions reduces the chances of this occurring, with also less chance of it occurring the more participants there are.
- **More participants needed** – as participants only do one condition each, they only generate one piece of data each. This means twice as many participants are needed as for an RMD (where each participant generates two pieces of data each) to generate the same amount of data.

Repeated measures design

With a repeated measures design, each participant does all of the conditions. In essence, participants are being tested against themselves. For example, Jenness (1932) got participants to individually estimate how many sweets there were in a jar before and after discussing it in a group. The IV was whether an estimate was made before discussing it in a group or afterwards, with the DV being how far their estimate was from the group estimate. Second individual estimates were closer to the group estimate, which suggested people are influenced by the presence of others in uncertain situations.

■ Strengths of the RMD

- **No group differences** – as each participant performs in every condition, there are no participant variables, which means it is easier to see the effect of the IV on the DV.
- **More data per participant** – as each participant performs in all conditions, more data per participant is generated than with an IGD. This means fewer participants are needed with an RMD compared to an IGD in order to generate the same amount of data.

Weaknesses of the RMD

- **Order effects** – as participants do all conditions, the order in which they do the conditions might affect the results. Participants may perform worse in the second condition due to fatigue or boredom (negative order effect), or they may perform better due to a learning/practice effect (positive order effect). However, order effects can be addressed by *counterbalancing*, where half the participants do condition A first followed by condition B, while half do condition B first followed by condition A. With counterbalancing, any order effects cancel each other out.
- **Demand characteristics** – as participants do all conditions, there is more opportunity for them to believe they have worked out the purpose of the study and alter their behaviour accordingly, which may confound the results.

Matched participants design

An MPD is a special kind of RMD. Different, but similar, participants are used in each condition, with participants matched on characteristics important to a specific study, such as age. Identical twins are often used for an MPD, as they form perfectly matched pairs. For example, Heydorn *et al.* (2003) used identical twins to investigate whether oxidized linalyl acetate (a common component of perfume) caused eczema. One of each twin pair had a perfume containing the substance put onto their skin and the other of each twin pair had a perfume put on their skin which did not contain the substance. Significantly more of the twins exposed to the substance developed eczema than those not exposed to it, which suggests it is linked to eczema.

Strengths of matched participants design

- **No order effects** – as different participants do each condition, there are no order effects.
- **Demand characteristics** – as participants only do one condition each, there is less opportunity for them to believe they have worked out the purpose of the study and alter their behaviour accordingly.
- **Group differences** – as participants are matched for similar important abilities, there should be less chance of participant variables (individual differences) confounding the results.

Weaknesses of matched participants design

- **More participants needed** – as each participant only does one condition, they only produce one piece of data each. Therefore, more participants are needed than for an RMD.
- **Time-consuming** – as matching requires pre-testing it is a relatively time-consuming process compared to the IGD and the RMD.
- **Matching is difficult** – it is difficult to match participants on all important variables, and, even when closely matched, individuals will still have different levels of motivation, fatigue, and so on. At any given moment in time that may confound results.

> **Expert tip**
>
> When selecting which experimental design to use for your experimental study, consider that, as order effects can generally be counterbalanced, the relative strengths of the RMD probably make it the best design to use to see the effects of the IV on the DV. However, if it is important or only possible for participants to do one condition of an experiment, an IGD would be preferable.

4 Mini-practicals

This section provides an explanation of and some ideas for mini-practicals that could be attempted as learning exercises to be undertaken before planning and carrying out your experimental study for the internal assessment. This includes advice on both descriptive and inferential statistical techniques.

On pages 78–82, there is a template that may prove useful to you in writing up any mini-practicals that you attempt. It is designed to mirror the sections of a conventional research report and so should give you some valuable experience of how to construct research reports before you embark upon writing up your actual experimental study.

A template has been filled in for the first mini-practical, based on Jacobs (1887) (see pages 24–27). Use this, if you wish, as a guide for how to fill in the template for the other suggested mini-practicals.

Although there is no formal requirement for you to conduct mini-practicals, they do give you some experience of planning, carrying out and writing up mini-practicals before you move on to the actual experimental study that will comprise the internal assessment.

If you do choose to have a go at conducting the mini-practicals, do not be afraid to make mistakes, as this is to be expected when you have little or no experience of conducting psychological research. Indeed, learning from mistakes is an extremely effective method of learning. Every time you make a mistake, as long as you understand why that mistake was made, something valuable is gained, and chances are you then will not repeat that mistake in the actual study done for the internal assessment.

The mini-practicals suggested here are simple ones, based upon actual research studies that correspond to psychological topics featured in the IB specification. You can use the template provided to record details of each study carried out, so it serves as a mini-practical report. It includes a section for the conducting of a suitable inferential statistical test to analyse the data generated from a study. If you wished, you could merely carry out a mini-practical as advised, with no requirement to fill in the template. Or you could omit whichever sections of the template you wished; for example, by not conducting an inferential statistical test.

The following two mini-practicals will be presented as worked examples, which could be used as 'first attempts' in conducting research. There will then be some further suggestions for which you should, at that point, be able to work out the finer details yourself. If at any point any terms used are not understood, then you should consult the 'Research methods' section in Chapter four of your psychology textbook (Lawton & Willard, 2018) before proceeding any further.

Jacobs (1887) mini-practical

An early psychology experiment was that of Jacobs (1887), who investigated the capacity of short-term memory (STM) with a method called the *serial digit span*. Participants were presented with increasingly long lists of single numbers or letters and had to recall them in the right order. Jacobs found that capacity for numbers was 9.3 items and for letters was 7.3. This is probably because there are fewer single digit numbers than letters in the alphabet; in other words, there are fewer numbers than letters to remember from. Jacobs omitted the number '7' and the letter 'W' as they are different in having not one but two syllables each, and so might have been more difficult to recall than single-syllable numbers and letters and may, therefore, have acted as an extraneous variable to confound the results. A one-tailed (directional) hypothesis is justified, as Jacob's findings suggest a direction of difference (that the longest sequence recalled will be greater for numbers than for letters).

To perform this study is simple and quick. However, as with all studies, careful initial preparation is necessary if it is to run smoothly and produce valid data. A repeated measures design (RMD) is used, where each participant is tested against themselves to determine their STM capacity for letters and numbers. The independent variable is whether numbers or letters are being presented and the dependent variable is the longest sequence recalled.

Aim

- To assess the capacity of STM for numbers and letters.

Hypotheses

Experimental (one-tailed):

- The longest sequence recalled will be significantly greater for numbers than for letters.

Null:

- There will be no significant difference in the longest sequence recalled for numbers and letters.

Materials

- A list of numbers and letters that have been randomly generated
- **Numbers:** 8, 6, 2, 1, 8, 3, 4, 2, 9, 5, 3, 6, 9, 2, 8
- **Letters:** F, A, P, Q, U, T, D, F, Z, R, S, P, T, F, M

Method

- Laboratory experiment

Design

- Repeated measures design

Procedure

- 10 participants, selected by opportunity sampling (those who are available), are read standardized instructions that clearly explain the purpose of the study and what will be expected of them (that they will be read a list of numbers or letters that increases in length and asked to recall it). At this point, they will be able to give (or not) their informed consent to take part in the study. They should also be reminded that they can withdraw from the study at any point.
- Each participant is tested individually and privately.

- The researcher reads out a single-digit number (e.g. '8') and the participant recalls it immediately aloud. The researcher then reads out a second single-digit number (e.g. '6') and the participant recalls both numbers in sequence aloud (i.e. '8, 6'). The researcher then reads out a third single-digit number (e.g. '2') and the participant recalls all three numbers in sequence aloud (i.e. '8, 6, 2'). The researcher continues reading out additional single-digit numbers and the participant recalls them in order until they make an error or cannot remember.
- The longest sequence of numbers correctly recalled is recorded.
- The procedure is repeated for letters.
- Numbers and letters used have been determined by random selection.
- The same sequence of numbers and letters used is the same for each participant.
- To deal with the possibility of order effects (where the order of presentation affects recall and so acts as an extraneous variable), *counterbalancing* is used, whereby half the participants are tested with numbers first and letters second, while half are tested with letters first and numbers second.
- Participants are thanked and debriefed. This should include telling them about the limited nature of STM capacity and that therefore their performance is quite usual.

Results

Descriptive:

Raw scores for the longest sequences recalled accurately by individual participants (which in a report would be found in the appendices):

Numbers: 10, 8, 7, 10, 9, 9, 8, 12, 9, 8

Letters: 7, 6, 5, 8, 8, 6, 6, 7, 9, 9

Findings should be presented in a results table (not a presentation of raw data). For example:

	Numbers	**Letters**
Total of the longest sequences recalled	90	71
Mean of the longest sequences recalled	9.0	7.1

Table 4.1 Table showing the total number and mean of the longest number and letter sequences recalled

Findings should also be presented as an appropriate graph (see page 23).

Findings should also be presented verbally in word form:

- *The total of the longest number of sequences recalled for numbers was 90, with a mean of 9.0 for the 10 participants. The total of the longest number of sequences recalled for letters was 71, with a mean of 7.1 for the 10 participants. The range of scores for numbers was 5, while the range of scores for letters was 4.*

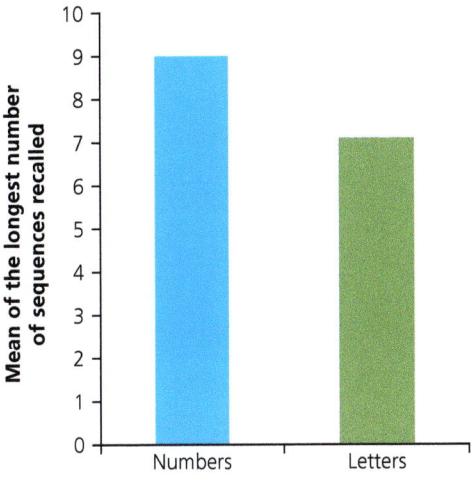

Figure 4.1 Bar chart showing mean of the longest number and letter sequences recalled

Inferential:

As an RMD has been used, with the data of at least ordinal (rankable) level and a difference between two conditions of an independent variable being sought, then a Wilcoxon signed-matched ranks test (see page 47) is appropriate.

The data is put into a table as follows with differences between pairs of scores ranked; no attention is paid to whether differences are plus (+) or minus (−), and scores of 'no difference' are omitted:

Highest number of sequences recalled for numbers	Highest number of sequences recalled for letters	Differences	Ranks
10	7	−3	7.5
8	6	−2	4.5
7	5	−2	4.5
10	8	−2	4.5
9	8	−1	1.5
9	6	−3	7.5
8	6	−2	4.5
12	7	−5	9
9	9	0	Omitted
8	9	+1	1.5

Table 4.2 Ranked difference table of highest number of number and letter sequences recalled

T = Sum of ranks for the less frequent sign (in this case the plus sign) = 1.

N = Number of ranked pairs = 9.

Critical value (cv) of T at the 0.05 significance level for a one-tailed test = 3 (found from a cv table).

T is significant as it is equal to or lower than the cv, therefore the null hypothesis can be rejected, and the experimental hypothesis accepted.

Conclusions

- STM capacity for numbers is greater than that for letters.
- STM capacity is limited.

Evaluation

- The experimental tasks of recalling lists of letters has little relevance to everyday activities and so lacks **ecological validity**.

> **Key definition**
> **Ecological validity** – the degree to which the findings from a study can be generalized to other settings.

Completed template for Jacobs (1887) mini-practical

Abstract

The aim of this laboratory experiment, based on the work of Jacobs (1887) into memory, was to see if there was a difference between short-term memory (STM) capacity for numbers and letters. Using a repeated measures design, counterbalanced for order effects, an opportunity sample of 10 participants had to repeat sequences of letters and numbers read aloud to them one at a time until they made a mistake. It was hypothesized that STM capacity would be greater for numbers and the results showed this to be true. It was concluded that STM capacity is finite, but greater for numbers than for letters.

Previous related research indicates

Jacobs (1887) investigated the capacity of STM with the serial digit span. Participants were presented with increasingly long lists of single numbers or letters and had to recall them in the right order. Jacobs found that capacity for numbers was 9.3 items and for letters was 7.3.

Research aims

- To assess the capacity of STM for numbers and letters.
- To assess whether STM capacity is between 5 and 9 items.

Hypotheses

Experimental (one-tailed):
The longest sequence recalled will be significantly greater for numbers than for letters.

Null:
There will be no significant difference in the longest sequence recalled for numbers and letters.

Brief description of research method and design

- Laboratory experiment, using a repeated measures design.
- Numbers: 8, 6, 2, 1, 8, 3, 4, 2, 9, 5, 3, 6, 9, 2, 8
- Letters: F, A, P, Q, U, T, D, F, Z, R, S, P, T, F, M
- 10 participants tested individually and privately.
- A participant immediately recalls aloud a number (or letter) said to them, then similarly recalls the first number (or letter) and a second one read to them and so on until they make an error.
- The longest amount of numbers (or letters) correctly recalled is recorded.
- The process is repeated for letters (or numbers).
- The order of presentation (letters or numbers) is counterbalanced to restrict order effects.

Sampling method and details

- An opportunity sample of 10 students who were available and willing were used.
- 5 females and 5 males.
- Aged 17–19.
- Participants were randomly assigned to recall either numbers or letters first.

IV

- The independent variable is whether numbers or letters are being presented and recalled.

DV

- The dependent variable is the longest sequence of numbers/letters recalled.

Ethical considerations
- Use of standardized instructions and consent forms to gain informed consent.
- No deceit present.
- Right to withdraw given.
- No harm was caused.
- Participants fully debriefed at the end of the study.

Pilot study indicated
- Numbers and letters weren't initially spoken clearly and loudly enough for participants to hear them.

Results table

	Numbers	Letters
Total of the longest sequences recalled	90	71
Mean of the longest sequences recalled	9.0	7.1

Graph

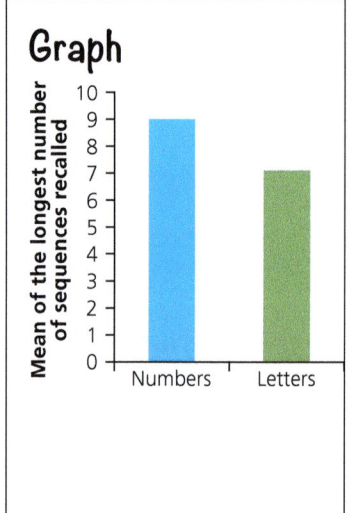

Verbal results summary
- The total of the longest sequences recalled for numbers was 90, with a mean of 9.0 for the 10 participants.
- The total of the longest sequences recalled for letters was 71, with a mean of 7.1 for the 10 participants.
- The range of scores for numbers was 12 – 7 = 5.
- The range of scores for letters was 9 – 5 = 4.

Inferential statistical test details
- A Wilcoxon signed-matched ranks test was used as the data was at least ordinal and an RMD was used.
- $T = 1$, $N = 9$.
- Level of significance = 0.05.
- cv for a one-tailed hypothesis = 3.
- Therefore, result is significant.

Hypothesis acceptance
- Accept the experimental one-tailed hypothesis.
- Reject the null hypothesis.

Evaluation
- The experimental tasks of recalling lists of letters and numbers has little relevance to everyday activities and so lacks ecological validity.
- Some numbers and letters were presented two or more times during the study, which could cause confusion and act as a confounding variable, invalidating the results.
- The study is ethical, as no deceit or harm is involved, informed consent was gained, the right to withdraw expressed and a full debriefing given at the end of the study.
- The findings have a practical application in using limited amounts of letters and numbers to form memorable postcodes for people's addresses.

Bruner and Postman (1947) mini-practical

The following mini-practical is based upon the study by Bruner and Postman (1947) into the idea of schema. A schema is a cognitive framework for structuring information about the physical world and the events and behaviour occurring within it. Put simply, humans perceive things not as they actually are, but how they expect them to be, based on available information, stereotypes and previous experience.

In the original study, participants were shown a picture of a white man and a black man arguing, with the white man brandishing a knife. However, on recall, participants generally remembered the black man as having the knife, due to the cultural stereotype at the time in the USA of black men being dangerous and carrying weapons. It was concluded, therefore, that schema does affect perception of events witnessed.

Figure 4.2 The knife often being inaccurately recalled as being held by the black man illustrates a type of recall error based on cultural stereotypes: Allport and Postman (1947)

Due to ethical problems of harm and social sensitivity in replicating the original experiment, the simplified version here uses different stimulus materials. Half of the participants will be shown briefly (for about 2 seconds) a card that has 'Paris in the the spring' written in a triangle on it, while half the participants will be shown a card (for the same amount of time) that has 'Glasgow in the summer' written similarly in a triangle on it (see Figure 4.3). Participants will then be asked to write down what they have seen, with the answer being judged either right or wrong. It is expected that participants will recall the 'Glasgow' card accurately, but that a significant number of participants in the 'Paris' condition will get it wrong by only recalling the word 'the' once, as that is what they expected to see.

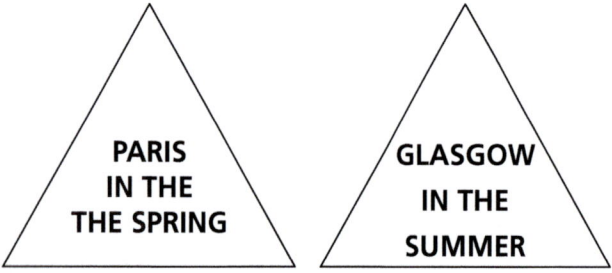

Figure 4.3 Paris and Glasgow cards

As this version of the study has not previously been reported, a two-tailed (non-directional) hypothesis is justifiable. As participants only do one condition each, an independent groups design (IGD) is being used. The independent variable is which card is witnessed (Paris or Glasgow) and the dependent variable is the number of correct responses. Filler statements could also be used to help reduce demand characteristics. For instance, all participants could be additionally shown other statements relating to famous cities, for example 'Belfast in the winter', and asked to recall them, but only the accuracy of the response to the 'Paris' or 'Glasgow' statement would be recorded.

Aim

- To assess whether schema affects recall of the wording of written statements witnessed.

Hypotheses

Experimental (two-tailed):

- There will be a significant difference in the number of statements accurately recalled between those witnessing 'Paris in the the spring' and those witnessing 'Glasgow in the summer'.

Null:

- There will be no significant difference in the number of statements accurately recalled between those witnessing 'Paris in the the spring' and those witnessing 'Glasgow in the summer'.

Method

- Laboratory experiment

Design

- Independent groups design

Materials

- 2 cards, each with a statement about a famous city written within a triangle on it: 1) 'Paris in the the spring' 2) 'Glasgow in the summer'
- Paper and pens to record participants' responses

Procedure

- Participants are read standardized instructions that clearly explain the purpose of the study and what will be expected of them (that they will be shown a statement and asked to recall it). At this point, they are able to give (or not) their informed consent to take part in the study. They should also be reminded that they can withdraw from the study at any point.
- 20 participants in total, who are allocated by random selection to each condition.
- Each participant is tested individually and privately.
- Half the participants (10) are shown the 'Paris' card for about 2 seconds and then asked to recall it by writing it down.
- Half of the participants (10) are shown the 'Glasgow' card for about 2 seconds and then asked to recall it by writing it down.

- The number of accurate responses is recorded for each condition.
- Participants are thanked and debriefed. This should include telling them about the idea of schema and that therefore their performance is quite usual.

Results

Descriptive:

Raw scores for whether stimulus was recalled accurately (which in a report would be found in the appendices):

- 'Paris in the the spring':   No, No, Yes, Yes, No, No, No, Yes, No, No
- 'Glasgow in the summer':   Yes, Yes, Yes, Yes, No, Yes, Yes, Yes, Yes, Yes

Findings should be presented in a results table (not a presentation of raw data). For example:

	'Paris' statement	'Glasgow' statement
Number of participants recalling statement accurately	3	9
Number of participants recalling statement inaccurately	7	1

Table 4.3 Table showing number of accurate and inaccurate responses to 'Paris' and 'Glasgow' statements

Findings should also be presented as an appropriate graph:

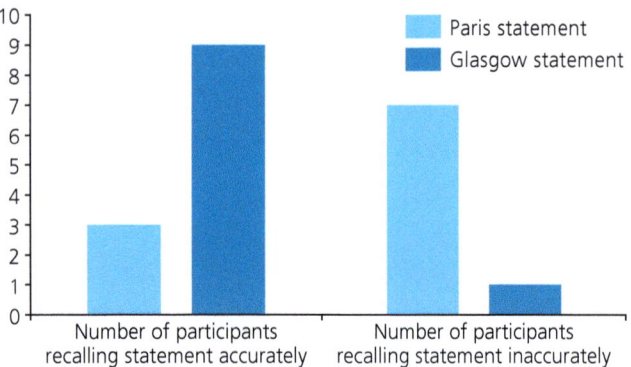

Figure 4.4 Bar chart showing number of accurate and inaccurate responses to 'Paris' and 'Glasgow' statements

Findings should also be presented verbally in word form:

- *3 participants correctly recalled the 'Paris' statement and 7 incorrectly. 9 participants correctly recalled the 'Glasgow' statement and 1 incorrectly.*

Inferential:

As an IGD has been used, with the data of nominal (frequency) level and a difference between two conditions of an independent variable being sought, then a chi-squared test is appropriate.

The data is put into a 2 × 2 contingency table (see Table 4.4 on page 31), with the expected frequencies (for there being no significant difference between the two conditions) calculated from the formula:

E = row total × column total ÷ by grand total

The chi-squared statistic is then calculated from the expected frequencies (E) and observed frequencies (O) using the formula:

$$\chi^2 = \Sigma(O - E - \tfrac{1}{2})^2 \div E$$

Condition	Paris		Glasgow		Row total	
Accurate recall	A	3	C	9		12
Inaccurate recall	B	7	D	1		8
Column total		10		10	GT	40

Table 4.4 Chi-squared contingency table

Row totals: 3 + 9 = 12 and 7 + 1 = 8

Column totals: 3 + 7 = 10 and 9 + 1 = 10

Grand total (GT): (10 + 10 + 12 + 8) = 40

Expected frequencies:

A: 12 × 10 ÷ 40 = 3
B: 8 × 10 ÷ 40 = 2
C: 12 × 10 ÷ 40 = 3
D: 8 × 10 ÷ 40 = 2

Calculate the difference between O and E for each cell:

A: 3 − 3 = 0
B: 7 − 2 = 5
C: 9 − 3 = 6
D: 1 − 2 = −1

Subtract $\frac{1}{2}$ for each $O - E$ value:

A: $0 - \frac{1}{2} = -0.5$
B: $5 - \frac{1}{2} = 4.5$
C: $6 - \frac{1}{2} = 5.5$
D: $-1 - \frac{1}{2} = -1.5$

Square this for each cell:

A: 0.5 × 0.5 = 0.25
B: 4.5 × 4.5 = 20.25
C: 5.5 × 5.5 = 30.25
D: −1.5 × −1.5 = 2.25

Divide each answer by the appropriate E value for that cell:

A: 0.25 ÷ 3 = 0.083
B: 20.25 ÷ 2 = 10.125
C: 30.25 ÷ 3 = 10.083
D: 2.25 ÷ 2 = 1.125

Calculate χ^2 by adding A + B + C + D = 0.083 + 10.125 + 10.083 + 1.125 = 21.416.

For χ^2 = 21.416 with 1 degree of freedom ($d.f.$) at the 0.05 level of significance for a two-tailed hypothesis, the critical value (cv) (taken from a critical value table) is 3.841.

As the value of χ^2 is equal to or exceeds the cv, a significant difference has been found; the null hypothesis can be rejected, and the two-tailed experimental hypothesis accepted.

> **Expert tip**
>
> The details from this study could be inserted into a copy of the mini-practical template, which will be good practice for your experimental study.

Additional mini-practicals

After completing two mini-practicals, you should now have some idea about what is required in the planning, carrying out and writing up of practical investigations, and hopefully have developed a degree of confidence in your ability to do so.

4 Mini-practicals

The following mini-practicals provide you with another opportunity to practise carrying out experiments if you feel it necessary. Each one gives some basic information, but it is up to you to work out the other necessary details, and possibly record the important points onto copies of the mini-practical template sheets.

Do not be afraid to make mistakes at this point – it will be a valuable learning experience to have before you progress onto undertaking your actual internal assessment. It is not important if these studies could be carried out or not as experiments for the internal assessment. What is important is to get some experience in planning and undertaking studies, including writing them up as mini-practicals.

■ Herlitz et al. (1997)

A quasi-experiment using an IGD, based on the study by Herlitz et al. (1997), who found that females outperformed males on tasks requiring episodic long-term memory, which suggests a gender difference in this type of LTM (see page 60 of Lawton & Willard, 2018).

> **■ ACTIVITY**
>
> Use Hertlitz's study to formulate suitable aims and hypotheses (a one-tailed experimental hypothesis could be justified due to the results of the study). You would also need to record relevant facts and conclusions drawn from Herlitz's study onto the 'Previous related research indicates' section of your mini-practical template. A minimum of about 10 males and 10 females will be needed to make the study representative and to allow statistical analysis to see if a real difference between genders exists (a difference that is beyond the boundaries of chance). Record details of your sampling method. Work out what the independent and dependent variables are, and record them on your mini-practical template (you will probably need these to help construct your aims and hypotheses).
>
> Construct suitable standardized instructions to be read to your participants. These should contain sufficient details so that participants can make a considered decision as to whether they wish to take part. What else will need to be in your standardized instructions? You will also need to write a descriptive passage concerning 20 episodic facts about your family (it does not have to be real facts). For example, 'my father is older than my mother' and 'I was born on a Sunday'. Participants are given this passage to read. Give them about 3 minutes to study the passage. Ask participants a question about each episodic fact contained in the passage and record how many each participant gets right. The participants should now be read a debriefing statement that fully explains the study, with an opportunity given for questions to be asked and answered.
>
> Once you have collected your data, it will be possible to construct a suitable table to record totals and means for females and males. The table should be fully titled and labelled. You will need to construct a suitable graph too that shows the differences between male and female scores. A verbal description of the results (in words) will also be needed.
>
> As an IGD has been used and the data is at least ordinal, with a difference being sought between two conditions, a chi-squared test could be used to analyse the data (a case could be made too for an independent t-test if the data is regarded as of interval level). After carrying out the test, the appropriate critical value will need to be decided through consideration of the level of significance used, how many degrees of freedom there are and whether your hypothesis was one- or two-tailed. It will then be possible to accept and reject hypotheses.
>
> Conclusions (relating to gender differences in episodic memory), relevant evaluative points and an idea for a future study suggested by the results could then be entered onto your mini-practical template.

> **Expert tip**
>
> A chi-squared test was calculated in the Bruner and Postman (1947) mini-practical, so refer to this and the section concerning chi-squared tests (see page 30) to calculate it in this instance.

Brochet and Dubourdieu (2001)

A laboratory experiment using an RMD based on the study by Brochet and Dubourdieu (2001), who found that expectation affected perceptual schema (see page 65 of Lawton & Willard, 2018), with expert wine tasters being fooled into believing that white wines dyed to look red were actually red wines (as that is what they expected them to taste like).

In the version suggested here, participants are tested individually and privately while blindfolded. In the first condition, they are given identical objects of equal weight to hold, one in each hand, with their hands outstretched (palms upwards) either side of their body. They are asked whether the objects are of the same or different weights and their responses are recorded. They are then asked to hold, with their arms outstretched on each side of the body again, a reasonably heavy object in one hand while simultaneously holding a much lighter object in the other hand. They should do this for about 30 seconds and then at the same time, with their arms still outstretched, the objects are replaced with the ones used originally. In this second condition, participants are again asked if the objects are of the same or different weights. Again, their responses are recorded.

If schema exerts an influence, then holding objects of equal weight in the second condition should actually feel to the participants as if they are holding objects of different weights. This is because of the expectation created by the effect on the muscles of the arms previously holding objects of unequal weights. The object placed into the hand that had the heavier weight in it should feel heavier than the object placed into the hand that held the lighter weight.

■ ACTIVITY

Compose suitable aims and hypotheses (a two-tailed experimental hypothesis could be appropriate, as this particular study has not been reported before, though a one-tailed experimental hypothesis could be justified by reference to Brochet and Dubourdieu's findings). You will need to record relevant facts and conclusions drawn from Brochet and Dubourdieu's study onto the 'Previous related research indicates' section of your mini-practical template. A minimum of 10 participants (who correctly judge in condition one that the objects are of equal weight) will be needed to make the study representative and to allow statistical analysis to see if a real difference between the two conditions exists (a difference that is beyond the boundaries of chance). Record details of your sampling method. Work out what the independent and dependent variables are and record them on your mini-practical template (you will probably need these to help construct your aims and hypotheses).

Construct suitable standardized instructions to be read to your participants. These should contain sufficient details so that participants can make a considered decision as to whether they wish to take part. You will especially need to explain, in order not to distress them, that their ability to assess weight is being assessed through touch and that is why they will need to be blindfolded. What else will need to be in your standardized instructions? At the end of the study, the participants should be read a debriefing statement that fully explains the study, with an opportunity given for questions to be asked and answered.

Once you have collected your data, it will be possible to construct a suitable table to record the total number of responses concerning whether participants believed the weights to be the same or different.

The table should be fully titled and labelled. You will need to construct a suitable graph too that shows the differences between responses in the two conditions. A verbal description of the results (in words) will also be needed.

As an RMD has been used and the data is nominal (occurs as frequencies), with a difference being sought between two conditions, a sign test would be used to analyse the data. Any participants who claim the two equal weights are actually different in condition one should not be included in the data.

A make-believe example version of the sign test for this study, which presumes eight participants say the objects in condition two are of different weight and two participants say they are of equal weight, is presented here to demonstrate how to conduct a sign test.

After carrying out the test, the appropriate critical value will need to be decided through consideration of the level of significance used and whether your hypothesis was one- or two-tailed. It will then be possible to accept and reject hypotheses.

Conclusions (relating to the effect of schema upon perception), relevant evaluative points and an idea for a future study suggested by the results could then be entered onto your mini-practical template.

■ Make-believe example of sign test for blindfolded object-holding study

Participant number	Equal weight or different	Direction of difference
1	Different	+
2	Different	+
3	Different	+
4	Different	+
5	Different	+
6	Different	+
7	Equal	−
8	Equal	−
9	Different	+
10	Different	+

Table 4.5 Table of results for calculating sign test

- s = the number of times the less frequent sign occurs = 2.
- cv for a two-tailed hypothesis and a 0.05 level of significance where N (the number of pairs of data) is 10 = 1.
- If s is less than or equal to the cv, reject the null hypothesis.
- As s in this instance is greater than the cv, the null hypothesis is accepted – this may seem strange when eight out of ten people incorrectly perceived the objects as being of unequal weight, but only ten participants were used, making it difficult for this test (which, as it only uses nominal data, isn't very sensitive in being able to detect significant differences when they do exist) to detect a significant difference. If more participants had been used and the same ratio of 'different' and 'equal' responses were recorded, then a significant difference would have been detected by the sign test.

■ Abernethy (1940)

A quasi-experiment using an IGD, which is based on the study by Abernethy (1940), who found that participants recalled information learned earlier better, if tested on it by a familiar person in the room where they learned the material, rather than being tested on it by an unfamiliar person in a different room to where they learned it. This suggested that if the context of coding (learning) of material differs from the context of retrieval (where information is recalled), then retrieval of the material will be negatively affected.

In the version suggested here, participants are read a statement that contains 20 facts, for example a name of someone, where they live, what their main hobby is, and so on. These shouldn't be too simple – you don't want everyone to get them all correct! Half the participants (selected randomly) remain in the room where the statement was read out with the researcher who read out the statement, while half the participants go to a different room with another researcher, who did not read out the statement and has not been seen by the participants up to this point.

Both groups are then asked an identical 20 questions concerning the 20 facts contained within the statement and write down their answers. The number of correct responses for each participant is recorded.

If the context of retrieval (the room in which testing occurs and familiarity with the researcher that tests them) acts as a cue for recall of information, then participants who are tested in the same room they heard the statement in by the same researcher who read it to them, should score significantly better than participants tested in a different room by a different researcher.

■ ACTIVITY

Compose suitable aims and hypotheses (a one-tailed experimental hypothesis could be justified by reference to Abernethy's findings). You will also need to record relevant facts and conclusions drawn from Abernethy's study onto the 'Previous related research indicates' section of your mini-practical template. About 20 participants will be needed to make the study representative and to allow statistical analysis to see if a real difference between the two conditions exists (a difference that is beyond the boundaries of chance). Record details of your sampling method. Work out what the independent and dependent variables are and record them on your mini-practical template (you will probably need these to help construct your aims and hypotheses).

Construct suitable standardized instructions to be read to your participants. These should contain sufficient details so that participants can make a considered decision as to whether they wish to take part. What else will need to be in your standardized instructions? At the end of the study, the participants should be read a debriefing statement that fully explains the study, with an opportunity given for questions to be asked and answered.

Once you have collected your data, it will be possible to construct a suitable table to record the total number of facts recalled in the two conditions, as well as mean scores.

The table should be fully titled and labelled. You will need to construct a suitable graph too that shows the differences between mean scores in the two conditions. A verbal description of the results (in words) will also be needed.

As an IGD has been used and the data is at least ordinal (rankable), with a difference being sought between two conditions, a Mann-Whitney test would be used to analyse the data (if the data is considered to be of interval level, then an independent t-test could be justified).

A make-believe example version of the Mann-Whitney test for this study, which presumes scores for participants, is presented here to demonstrate how to conduct a Mann-Whitney test.

After carrying out the test, the appropriate critical value will need to be decided through consideration of the level of significance used and whether your hypothesis was one- or two-tailed. It will then be possible to accept and reject hypotheses.

Conclusions (relating to the effect of context of retrieval acting as a cue for recall), relevant evaluative points and an idea for a future study suggested by the results can then be entered onto your mini-practical template.

Make-believe example of Mann-Whitney test for context of retrieval

Group A: Participants tested in same room	Score on test of recall	Rank	Group B: Participants tested in different room	Score on test of recall	Rank
1	15	20	11	5	1
2	12	16	12	6	2.5
3	12	16	13	7	4.5
4	14	19	14	9	8.5
5	10	11	15	11	13.5
6	11	13.5	16	12	16
7	13	18	17	6	2.5
8	8	6.5	18	8	6.5
9	10	11	19	7	4.5
10	9	8.5	20	10	11

Table 4.6 Table of results for calculation of Mann-Whitney test

- For the calculation of T we need to know N_A (the sum of scores in the smaller sample or, as here, if both samples are of equal size, the sum of the samples in group A) = 139.5.
- Then, to find U, multiply N_A by N_B = 10 × 10 = 100.
- Add this number to $N_A \times (N_A + 1) \div 2 - T$.
- $U = 100 + (110 \div 2) - 139.5$
- $U = 155 - 139.5$
- $U = 15.5$
- Then, find $U' = N_A \times N_B - U$.
- $U' = 100 - 15.5$
- $U' = 84.5$
- Look up the smaller of U and U' in a critical value table.
- The cv for a one-tailed hypothesis with a 0.05 significance level, where N_A = 10 and N_B = 10 is 23.
- If U is equal to or less than the cv, it is significant.
- Therefore, reject the null hypothesis and accept the experimental one-tailed hypothesis.

Further practice

You might now find it useful to go through your textbook (Lawton & Willard, 2018), or other sources of psychology research studies available to you, and think about how these studies might actually be carried out, what sort of practical problems they present in doing so and how such problems could be overcome.

Try to also consider what extraneous variables need to be controlled so that the effect of the independent variable upon the dependent variable would be being measured and not some other variable. You may even feel confident enough at this point to actually attempt one or two of these studies to see how you cope with these challenges, filling in the details onto a mini-practical template as you do.

5 Descriptive and inferential statistical analysis

Data generated from your experimental study will need to be subjected to descriptive statistical and inferential statistical analysis. Details of these analyses will be recorded in the analysis section of your research report.

Descriptive statistical analysis

Descriptive statistics describe the data numerically in table form, visually in the form of a graph and verbally in the form of a written description.

- **Tables** – summarize the main findings of data and thus differ from data tables which just present raw, unprocessed scores from studies. Totals, percentages and relevant measures of central tendency (means, medians and modes) and dispersion (range and standard deviation) can be presented. Tables need to be clearly and fully titled and labelled.
- **Graphs** – allow patterns in data to be easily seen. There are four main types used with data from experimental studies:
  1 *Bar charts* – show data in the form of the separate categories being compared. The bars do not touch to show that data are not continuous (come from separate categories). Categories are placed on the *x*-(horizontal) axis and scores on the *y*-(vertical) axis. Bar charts can show totals, means, ratios, percentages and even two values together (like chocolate consumption by age and gender).

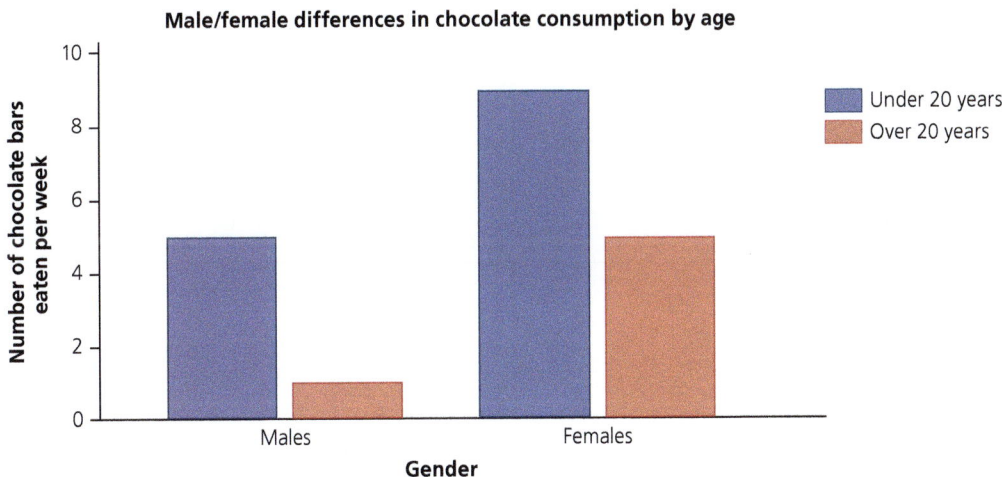

Figure 5.1 Bar chart

2 *Histograms* – show data are continuous (from the same category), which is why the bars touch. Continuous scores go on the *x*-axis and frequency of scores goes on the *y*-axis.

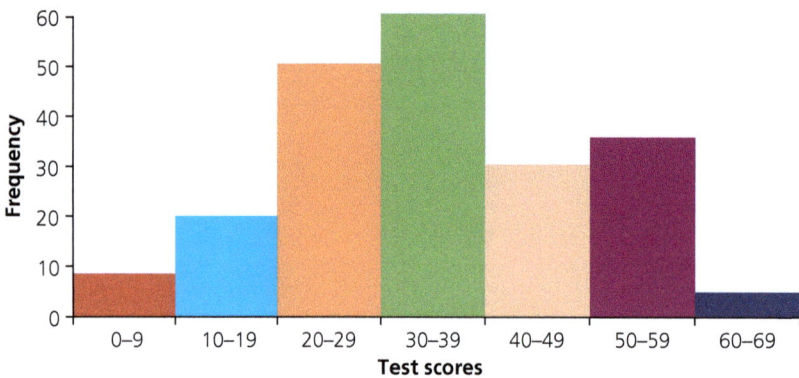

Figure 5.2 Histogram

3 *Frequency polygons (line graphs)* – similar to histograms, as data on the *x*-axes are continuous (from the same category). The graph is produced by drawing a line from the mid-point top of each bar in a histogram. This permits two or more frequency distributions to be shown on the same graph.

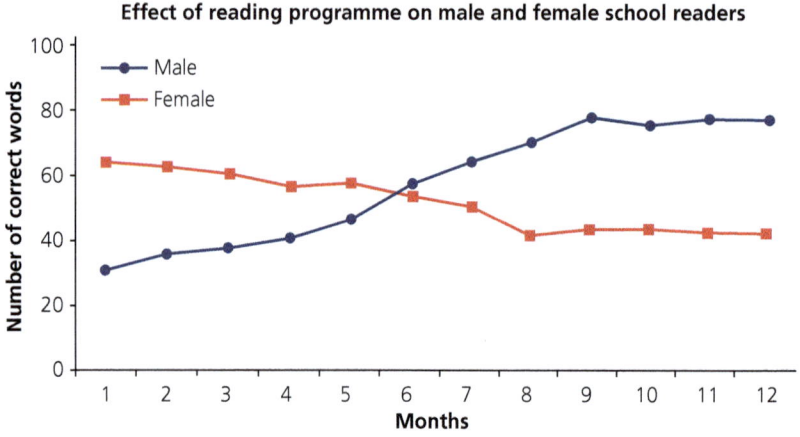

Figure 5.3 Frequency polygon

4 *Pie charts* – show the frequency of categories as percentages. The 'pie' is split into sections, each one representing the frequency of a category. Sections are colour-coded with a grid given to show what each section represents.

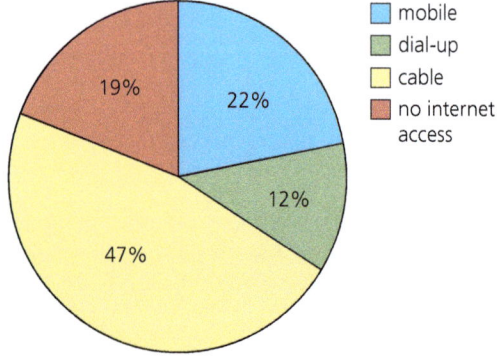

Figure 5.4 Pie chart

Inferential statistical tests for experiments

This section provides a description and explanation of inferential statistical analysis for experiments. This will help you to understand:

1. The purpose of inferential statistical analysis in the scientific process
2. Which tests to choose for different experimental research settings
3. The procedures involved for carrying out individual tests.

Descriptive statistical analysis does exactly what it suggests; it describes the findings in numerical (table), visual (graph) and verbal (words) forms (see 'Descriptive statistical analysis', page 37). However, inferential statistical analysis is more complex and sophisticated. It involves the use of statistical tests to assess, in the case of experiments, whether measured differences between two conditions of an independent variable are *significant differences* (beyond the boundaries of chance) that can be generalized from the sample tested to the whole target population that the sample represents.

If a coin is tossed 100 times, then by the law of averages there should be 50 heads and 50 tails. However, it might be 52 heads and 48 tails, which means there is a difference between the two sets of data (52 and 48), but is it beyond the boundaries of chance for that to occur? Would you suspect something was amiss, like the coin being weighted on one side or that the person tossing the coin was manipulating it in some way? Probably not. But where would you 'draw the line' between a result being within chance factors and falling outside them? 60 heads and 40 tails? 90 heads and 10 tails? This is what inferential statistical tests do, they use the concept of *probability*, through the use of statistical calculations, to set a 'cut-off point' that determines if differences between sets of experimental data are 'real' (significant) differences beyond the boundaries of chance.

■ Probability

Probability concerns how certain researchers are that a difference between two sets of data is a 'real' (significant) difference. There is no such thing as absolute certainty (100% probability) that a difference was not due to chance factors. There is a slight possibility that debris from space, hurtling through the atmosphere, will strike you dead in the next few seconds; it probably won't happen, but there is a slight possibility that it could happen.

This is why in science it is impossible to 'prove' something beyond all doubt. Therefore, we need a 'cut-off' point beyond which we will accept a statistical test result as showing a significant difference.

In psychology, a significance (probability) level of 5% is used, which is expressed as:

$p \leq 0.05$

This means that there is a 5% possibility that an observed difference between two sets of data (such as that between a coin landing heads or tails when tossed), which is said by an inferential statistical test to be 'significant' (beyond the boundaries of chance), is actually due to chance factors. This means the null hypothesis would be wrongly rejected and the experimental hypothesis wrongly accepted. This phenomenon is known as a *Type I error*, for example when a pregnancy test says a woman is pregnant and she isn't. This is regarded in psychology as being an acceptable level of error. With a 5% significance level, it means that, on average, for every 100 significant differences found by inferential statistical tests, where the null hypothesis would be rejected, 5 of them would be wrong.

When experimenting in new research areas that haven't been explored before (or when testing potentially harmful stimuli, like newly manufactured drugs), it is customary to use a stricter, higher level of significance, such as a 1% significance level, which is expressed as:

$p \leq 0.01$

This means there is only a 1% possibility that an observed difference between two sets of data, said by an inferential test to be 'significant' is actually due to chance factors. An even stricter level of significance of $p \leq 0.001$ would mean there's a 99.9% certainty of an observed difference between two sets of data being beyond chance factors, but there would still be a 0.1% chance that the difference had occurred by chance.

There is a possibility when using strict levels of significance (such as a 1% level) that no significant difference will be found by an inferential statistical test, when in fact the observed difference was actually beyond chance factors, such as a pregnancy test saying a woman isn't pregnant when in fact she is. This would mean that the null hypothesis would be wrongly accepted and the experimental hypothesis wrongly rejected. This is called a *Type II error*. The stricter the level of significance used, the more chance there is of a Type II error occurring.

The reason a 5% significance level is used as the 'accepted level' in psychological research, is because it is seen as striking a balance between making a Type I and a Type II error.

■ Interpretation of significance

Inferential statistical tests produce an *observed value*, which is then compared to a critical value (*cv*) in a critical value table in order to determine if the observed value is significant and thus whether hypotheses can be accepted or rejected. What an actual *cv* will be depends upon whether an experimental hypothesis is one- or two-tailed (also known as directional and non-directional), the number of participants or participant pairs (*N*) used and what level of significance (usually the 5% level) is used.

The actual interpretations of observed and critical values of specific statistical tests will be referenced when detailing individual tests.

■ Choosing specific inferential statistical tests for experimental studies

Once an experiment has been carried out and data generated, an appropriate inferential statistical test must be selected. Choice of test, other than the fact that to analyse data generated from experiments requires a test of difference, is dependent on two factors:

1. *The experimental design used* – whether an independent group design (each participant only does one condition of the experiment) or repeated measures design (each participant does all conditions of the experiment) was used (a matched participants design is regarded as a type of repeated measures design).
2. *The level of data generated* – whether the data is of **nominal, ordinal** or **interval/ratio** level.

> **Key definitions**
>
> **Nominal data** – a crude, relatively uninformative level of data that involves frequencies, e.g. how many people prefer orange juice or lemonade.
>
> **Ordinal data** – a more informative level of data that involves data which are rankable (can be put into rank order), e.g. the finishers in a running race. Data that is ordinal is also of nominal level.
>
> **Interval/ratio data** – the most informative level of data that involves data of equal measurement intervals, e.g. seconds in time. Interval data has an arbitrary zero point, whereas ratio data has an absolute zero point. For instance, temperature is interval as there can be a minus reading (e.g. minus 15 degrees centigrade), while someone with zero pounds in their bank account has no money (ratio data). Data that is interval/ratio is also of nominal and ordinal level.

Once the experimental design and data levels have been determined, consult Table 5.1 for choice of appropriate test.

	Independent groups design	Repeated measures design
Nominal data	Chi-squared test	Sign test
Ordinal data	Mann-Whitney test	Wilcoxon signed-matched ranks test
Interval/ratio data	Independent t-test	Repeated t-test

Table 5.1 Inferential statistical tests

Tests based on nominal level data (chi-squared and sign test) are less sensitive (due to the uninformative nature of the data), which means that these tests are less able than more sensitive tests to detect a significant difference if there is one (and therefore make it easier to make a Type II error and wrongly accept a null hypothesis).

Tests based on ordinal level data (Mann-Whitney and Wilcoxon signed-matched ranks) are more sensitive (due to the more informative nature of the data) and so are more able to detect a significant difference if there is one (and thus less likely to lead to a Type II error and a null hypothesis being wrongly accepted). However, tests based on interval/ratio data (independent t-test and repeated t-test) are the most sensitive and thus most able to detect a significant difference if there is one (and thus least likely to lead to a Type II error and a null hypothesis being wrongly accepted).

The sign test

Criteria for choice

The sign test is used when a repeated measures design (RMD) has been used and the data is of at least nominal level.

Rationale of the test

The test compares the number of scores that go in one direction (e.g. prefer orange juice) to the number of scores that go in another direction (e.g. prefer lemonade) to see if any difference in direction of scores is beyond chance factors (is 'significant').

How to calculate the sign test

- Put the data into appropriate table form (see 'Make-believe example of sign test for blindfolded object-holding study', page 34).
- A plus (+) sign is put next to scores that go in one direction and a minus sign (−) to scores that go in the other direction (see Make-believe example).
- s = the number of times the less frequent sign occurs.
- Find the cv from an appropriate critical value table – this will be dependent on whether a one- or two-tailed hypothesis (directional or non-directional) has been used and the number of pairs of data used (N).
- If s is less than or equal to the cv, reject the null hypothesis.

Level of significance for a two-tailed test				
	0.05	0.025	0.01	0.005
Level of significance for a one-tailed test				
N	0.10	0.05	0.02	0.01
5	0	–	–	–
6	0	0	–	–
7	0	0	0	–
8	1	0	0	0
9	1	1	0	0
10	1	1	0	0
11	2	1	1	0
12	2	2	1	1
13	3	2	1	1
14	3	2	2	1
15	3	3	2	2
16	4	3	2	2
17	4	4	3	2
18	5	4	3	3
19	5	4	4	3
20	5	5	4	3

Table 5.2 Levels of significance for one- and two-tailed tests

The chi-squared test

Criteria for choice

The chi-squared test is used when an independent groups design (IGD) has been used and the data is of at least nominal level.

Rationale of the test

The test compares the expected frequencies of scores to the actual observed frequencies to see if they differ beyond chance factors. For example, comparing how many people accurately recalled a written statement about Paris with how many people accurately recalled a written statement about Glasgow (see page 28). If there is no significant difference between the frequency of the scores, then the expected frequencies should be similar to the observed frequencies.

How to calculate the chi-squared test

- Put the observed scores into a 2 × 2 contingency table, with the four cells referred to as A, B, C and D (see Table 4.4, page 31).

	Condition one	Condition two	Row total
First frequency	Cell A	Cell C	
Second frequency	Cell B	Cell D	
Column total			GT

Table 5.3 Chi-squared contingency table

- Calculate the expected frequencies (E) for each cell (A, B, C and D) from:

  E = row total × column total ÷ grand total

- The chi-squared (χ^2) statistic is then calculated from the expected frequencies (E) and observed frequencies (O) using the formula:

  $\chi^2 = \Sigma(O - E - \frac{1}{2})^2 \div E$

- See calculations for chi-squared test for the Bruner and Postman (1947) mini-practical, page 30.

- Find the *cv* from an appropriate critical value table – this will be dependent on whether you have a one- or two-tailed hypothesis (directional or non-directional), the level of significance used and the degrees of freedom (d.f.) (which with a 2 × 2 contingency table is 1).

- If χ^2 is equal to or greater than the *cv*, it is significant and so reject the null hypothesis.

d.f.	0.20	0.10	0.05	0.02	0.01	0.001
1	1.64	2.71	3.84	5.41	6.64	10.83
2	3.22	4.6	5.99	7.82	9.21	13.82
3	4.64	6.25	7.82	9.84	11.34	16.27
4	5.99	7.78	9.49	11.67	13.28	18.46
5	7.29	9.24	11.07	13.39	15.09	20.52
6	8.56	10.64	12.59	15.03	16.81	22.46
7	9.8	12.02	14.07	16.62	18.48	24.32
8	11.03	13.36	15.51	18.17	20.09	26.12
9	12.24	14.68	16.92	19.68	21.67	27.88
10	13.44	15.99	18.31	21.16	23.21	29.59
11	14.63	17.28	19.68	22.62	24.72	31.26
12	15.81	18.55	21.03	24.05	26.22	32.91
13	16.98	19.81	22.36	25.47	27.69	34.53
14	18.15	21.06	23.68	26.87	29.14	36.12
15	19.31	22.31	25.0	28.26	30.58	37.7
16	20.46	23.54	26.3	29.63	32.0	39.29
17	21.62	24.77	27.59	31.0	33.41	40.75
18	22.76	25.99	28.87	32.35	34.8	42.31
19	23.9	27.2	30.14	33.69	36.19	43.82
20	25.04	28.41	31.41	35.02	37.57	45.32
21	26.17	29.62	32.67	36.34	38.93	46.8
22	27.3	30.81	33.92	37.66	40.29	48.27
23	28.43	32.01	35.17	38.97	41.64	49.73
24	29.55	33.2	36.42	40.27	42.98	51.18
25	30.68	34.38	37.65	41.57	44.31	52.62
26	31.8	35.56	38.88	42.86	45.64	54.05
27	32.91	36.74	40.11	44.14	46.96	55.48
28	34.03	37.92	41.34	45.42	48.28	56.89
29	35.14	39.09	42.69	46.69	49.59	58.3
30	36.25	40.26	43.77	47.96	50.89	59.7

Table 5.4 Critical values of chi-squared for a two-tailed (non-directional) test. Chi-squared is significant if it is equal to or greater than the table value

d.f.	0.10	0.05	0.025	0.01	0.005	0.0005
1	1.64	2.71	3.84	5.41	6.64	10.83

Table 5.5 Critical values of chi-squared for a one-tailed (directional) test

The Mann-Whitney test

Criteria for choice

The Mann-Whitney test is used when an independent groups design has been used and the data is of at least ordinal level.

Rationale of the test

The test compares the ranks of two sets of data to see if they differ significantly from each other. If they do not, then the totals of the ranks of the two sets of data should be similar. For example, ranking the scores of people who sat a test in the room where they learned the information against people who sat the test in a different room, and then seeing if the total of the ranks for one condition is significantly different from that of the other condition (see page 34).

How to calculate the Mann-Whitney test

- Construct an appropriate table for calculating a Mann-Whitney test.

Participants Condition A:	Score	Rank	Participants Condition B:	Score	Rank
1			11		
2			12		
3			13		
4			14		
5			15		
6			16		
7			17		
8			18		
9			19		
10			20		

Table 5.6 Table for calculation of Mann-Whitney test

- Insert data into table, calculate ranks and insert into table (see 'Make-believe example of Mann-Whitney test for context of retrieval', page 36).
- Find the sum of ranks for the smaller sample (T). If both samples are of equal size, find the sum of the samples in condition A.
- Then, to find U, multiply N_A by N_B = 10 × 10 = 100, where N_A is the number of participants in condition A and N_B is the number of participants in condition B.
- Add this number to $N_A \times (N_A + 1) \div 2 - T$
- Then find $U' = N_A \times N_B - U$
- The smaller of U and U' is compared to the *cv*.
- Find the *cv* from an appropriate critical value table – this will be dependent on whether you have a one- or two-tailed hypothesis (directional or non-directional), the level of significance used and the value of N (the number of ranked pairs).
- If the smaller of U and U' is equal to or less than the *cv*, it is significant, and the null hypothesis can be rejected.

	1	2	3	4	5	6	7	8	9	10	11	12	13	14	15	16	17	18	19	20
1	–	–	–	–	–	–	–	–	–	–	–	–	–	–	–	–	–	–	–	–
2	–	–	–	–	–	–	–	–	–	–	–	–	–	–	–	–	–	–	–	–
3	–	–	–	–	–	–	–	–	0	0	0	1	1	1	2	2	2	2	3	3
4	–	–	–	–	–	0	0	1	1	2	2	3	3	4	5	5	6	6	7	8
5	–	–	–	–	0	1	1	2	3	4	5	6	7	7	8	9	10	11	12	13
6	–	–	–	0	1	2	3	4	5	6	7	9	10	11	12	13	15	16	17	18
7	–	–	–	0	1	3	4	6	7	9	10	12	13	15	16	18	19	21	22	24
8	–	–	–	1	2	4	6	7	9	11	13	15	17	18	20	22	24	26	28	30
9	–	–	0	1	3	5	7	9	11	13	16	18	20	22	24	27	29	31	33	36
10	–	–	0	2	4	6	9	11	13	16	18	21	24	26	33	31	34	37	39	42
11	–	–	0	2	5	7	10	13	16	18	21	24	27	30	39	36	39	42	45	48
12	–	–	1	3	6	9	12	15	18	21	24	27	31	34	37	41	44	47	51	54
13	–	–	1	3	7	10	13	17	20	24	27	31	34	38	42	45	49	53	56	60
14	–	–	1	4	7	11	15	18	22	26	31	34	38	42	46	50	54	58	63	67
15	–	–	2	5	8	12	16	20	24	29	34	37	42	46	51	55	60	64	69	73
16	–	–	2	5	9	13	18	22	27	31	36	41	45	50	55	60	65	70	74	79
17	–	–	2	6	10	15	19	24	29	34	39	44	49	54	60	65	70	75	81	86
18	–	–	2	6	11	16	21	26	31	37	42	47	53	58	64	70	75	81	87	92
19	–	0	3	7	12	17	22	28	33	39	45	51	56	63	69	74	81	87	93	99
20	–	0	3	8	13	18	24	30	36	42	58	54	60	67	73	79	86	92	99	105

Table 5.7 Mann-Whitney: Critical value table of U for a one-tailed (directional) test at $p = 0.005$ and two-tailed (non-directional) test at $p = 0.01$. Dashes indicate no decision is possible at the stated level of significance. For any $N1$ and $N2$, the observed value of U will be significant if it is equal to or less than the critical values shown

	1	2	3	4	5	6	7	8	9	10	11	12	13	14	15	16	17	18	19	20
1	–	–	–	–	–	–	–	–	–	–	–	–	–	–	–	–	–	–	–	–
2	–	–	–	–	–	–	–	–	–	–	–	–	0	0	0	0	0	0	1	1
3	–	–	–	–	–	–	0	0	1	1	1	2	2	2	3	3	4	4	4	5
4	–	–	–	–	0	1	1	2	3	3	4	5	5	6	7	7	8	9	9	10
5	–	–	–	0	1	2	3	4	5	6	7	8	9	10	11	12	13	14	15	16
6	–	–	–	1	2	3	4	6	7	8	9	11	12	13	15	16	18	19	20	22
7	–	–	0	1	3	4	6	7	9	11	12	14	16	17	19	21	23	24	26	28
8	–	–	0	2	4	6	7	9	11	13	15	17	20	22	24	26	28	30	32	34
9	–	–	1	3	5	7	9	11	14	16	18	21	23	26	28	31	3	36	38	40
10	–	–	1	3	6	8	11	13	16	19	22	24	27	30	33	36	38	41	44	47
11	–	–	1	4	7	9	12	15	18	22	25	28	31	34	37	41	44	47	50	53
12	–	–	2	5	8	11	14	17	21	24	28	31	35	38	42	46	49	53	56	60
13	–	0	2	5	9	12	16	20	23	27	31	35	39	43	47	51	55	59	63	67
14	–	0	2	6	10	13	17	22	26	30	34	38	43	47	51	56	60	65	69	73
15	–	0	3	7	11	15	19	24	28	33	37	42	47	51	56	61	66	70	75	80
16	–	0	3	7	12	16	21	26	31	36	41	46	51	56	61	66	71	76	82	87
17	–	0	4	8	13	18	23	28	33	38	43	49	55	60	66	71	77	82	88	93
18	–	0	4	9	14	19	24	30	36	41	47	53	59	65	70	76	82	88	94	100
19	–	1	4	9	15	20	26	32	38	44	50	56	63	69	75	82	88	94	101	107
20	–	1	5	10	16	22	28	34	40	47	53	60	67	73	80	87	93	100	107	114

Table 5.8 Mann-Whitney: Critical value table of U for a one-tailed (directional) test at $p = 0.01$ and two-tailed (non-directional) test at $p = 0.02$. Dashes indicate no decision is possible at the stated level of significance. For any $N1$ and $N2$, the observed value of U will be significant if it is equal to or less than the critical values shown

	1	2	3	4	5	6	7	8	9	10	11	12	13	14	15	16	17	18	19	20
1	–	–	–	–	–	–	–	–	–	–	–	–	–	–	–	–	–	–	–	–
2	–	–	–	–	–	–	–	–	–	–	–	–	0	0	0	0	0	0	1	1
3	–	–	–	–	0	1	1	2	2	3	3	4	4	5	5	6	6	7	7	8
4	–	–	–	0	1	2	3	4	4	5	6	7	8	9	10	11	11	12	13	13
5	–	–	0	1	2	3	5	6	7	8	9	11	12	13	14	15	17	18	19	20
6	–	–	0	1	3	5	6	7	8	10	11	13	14	16	17	19	21	22	25	27
7	–	–	1	3	5	6	8	10	12	14	16	18	20	22	24	26	28	30	32	34
8	–	0	2	4	6	8	10	13	15	17	19	22	24	26	29	31	34	36	38	41
9	–	0	2	4	7	10	12	15	17	20	23	26	28	31	34	37	39	42	45	48
10	–	0	3	5	8	11	14	17	20	23	26	29	33	36	39	42	45	48	52	55
11	–	0	3	6	9	13	16	19	23	26	30	33	37	40	44	47	51	55	58	62
12	–	1	4	7	11	14	18	22	26	29	33	37	41	45	49	55	57	61	65	69
13	–	1	4	8	12	16	20	24	28	33	37	41	45	50	54	59	63	67	74	76
14	–	1	5	9	13	17	22	26	31	36	40	45	50	55	59	64	67	74	78	83
15	–	1	5	10	14	19	24	29	34	39	44	49	54	59	64	70	76	80	85	90
16	–	1	6	11	15	21	26	31	37	42	47	53	59	64	70	75	81	86	92	98
17	–	2	6	11	17	22	28	34	39	45	51	57	63	67	75	81	87	93	99	105
18	–	2	7	12	18	24	30	36	42	48	55	61	67	74	80	86	93	99	106	112
19	–	2	7	13	19	25	32	38	45	52	58	65	72	78	85	92	99	106	113	119
20	–	2	8	13	20	27	34	41	48	55	62	69	76	83	90	98	105	112	119	127

Table 5.9 Mann-Whitney: Critical value table of U for a one-tailed (directional) test at $p = 0.025$ and two-tailed (non-directional) test at $p = 0.05$. Dashes indicate no decision is possible at the stated level of significance. For any N1 and N2, the observed value of U will be significant if it is equal to or less than the critical values shown

	1	2	3	4	5	6	7	8	9	10	11	12	13	14	15	16	17	18	19	20
1	–	–	–	–	–	–	–	–	–	–	–	–	–	–	–	–	–	–	0	0
2	–	–	–	–	0	0	0	1	1	1	1	2	2	2	3	3	3	4	4	4
3	–	–	0	0	1	2	2	3	3	4	5	5	6	7	7	8	9	9	10	11
4	–	–	0	1	2	3	4	5	6	7	8	9	10	11	12	14	15	16	17	18
5	–	0	1	2	4	5	6	8	9	11	12	13	15	16	18	19	20	22	23	25
6	–	0	2	3	5	7	8	10	12	14	16	17	19	21	23	25	26	28	30	32
7	–	0	2	4	6	8	11	13	15	17	19	21	24	26	28	30	33	35	37	39
8	–	1	3	5	8	10	13	15	18	20	23	26	28	31	33	36	39	41	44	47
9	–	1	3	6	9	12	15	18	21	24	27	30	33	36	39	42	45	48	51	54
10	–	1	4	7	11	14	17	20	24	27	31	34	37	41	44	48	51	54	58	62
11	–	1	5	8	12	16	19	23	27	31	34	38	42	46	50	54	57	61	65	69
12	–	2	5	9	13	17	21	26	30	34	38	42	47	51	55	60	64	68	72	77
13	–	2	6	10	15	19	24	28	33	37	42	47	51	56	61	65	70	75	80	84
14	–	2	7	11	16	21	26	31	36	41	46	51	56	61	66	71	77	82	87	92
15	–	3	7	12	18	23	28	33	39	44	50	55	61	66	72	77	83	88	94	100
16	–	3	8	14	19	25	30	36	42	48	54	60	65	71	77	83	89	95	101	107
17	–	3	9	15	20	26	33	39	45	51	57	64	70	77	83	89	96	102	109	115
18	–	4	9	16	22	28	35	41	48	55	61	68	75	82	88	95	102	109	116	123
19	–	4	10	17	23	30	37	44	51	58	65	72	80	87	94	101	109	116	123	130
20	–	4	11	18	25	32	39	47	54	62	69	77	84	92	100	107	115	123	130	138

Table 5.10 Mann-Whitney: Critical value table of U for a one-tailed (directional) test at $p = 0.05$ and two-tailed (non-directional) test at $p = 0.10$. Dashes indicate no decision is possible at the stated level of significance. For any N1 and N2, the observed value of U will be significant if it is equal to or less than the critical values shown

The Wilcoxon signed-matched ranks test

Criteria for choice
- The Wilcoxon signed-matched ranks test is used when a repeated measures design has been used and the data is of at least ordinal level.

Rationale of the test
- The test ascertains whether there is a significant difference in paired observations (measurements taken from the same participant). Differences in pairs of scores are ranked according to their size, with the sum of the ranks of the less frequent sign (positive or negative differences) assessed to see whether it differs significantly from a critical value. For example, seeing whether there is a significant difference in the highest number of sequences recalled for letters compared to numbers when both have been assessed in participants (see the Jacobs (1887) mini-practical, page 23).

How to calculate the Wilcoxon signed-matched ranks test
- Construct an appropriate table for the calculation of a Wilcoxon signed-matched ranks test.

Participants' scores for the first condition of the IV	Participants' scores for the second condition of the IV	Differences between scores	Ranks of scores

Table 5.11 Table for the calculation of a Wilcoxon signed-matched ranks test

- Data is put into the table with differences between pairs of scores ranked (with no attention paid to whether differences are plus (+) or minus (−)) and scores of 'no difference' omitted (see table for Jacobs (1887) mini-practical, page 23).
- Calculate T, which is the sum of ranks for the less frequent sign (either minus or positive).
- Find the cv from an appropriate critical value table – this will be dependent on whether you have a one- or two-tailed hypothesis (directional or non-directional), the level of significance used and the value of N (the number of ranked pairs).
- Compare T to the cv.
- If T is equal to or lower than the cv, there is a significant difference and the null hypothesis can be rejected.

	Level of significance for a two-tailed (directional) hypothesis			
	0.10	0.05	0.02	0.01
	Level of significance for a one-tailed (non-directional) hypothesis			
N	0.05	0.025	0.01	0.005
5	0			
6	2	0		
7	3	2	0	
8	5	3	1	0
9	8	5	3	1
10	10	8	5	3
11	13	10	7	5
12	17	13	9	7
13	21	17	12	9
14	25	21	15	12
15	30	25	19	15
16	35	29	23	19
17	41	34	27	23
18	47	40	32	27
19	53	46	37	32
20	60	52	43	37
21	67	58	49	42
22	75	65	55	48
23	83	73	62	54
24	91	81	69	61
25	100	89	76	68

Table 5.12 Critical values of T for the Wilcoxon signed-matched ranks test. Values of T that are equal to or less than the table value are significant

The independent t-test

Criteria for choice

The independent t-test is used when an independent groups design has been used and the data is of interval/ratio level.

Rationale of the test

The test compares the size of the differences in the mean scores of two sets of data drawn from independent (non-related) sources to see if they differ significantly from each other. For example, to see if the score on a test done by participants having no sleep last night differs significantly from those doing the test after eight hours' sleep last night (see page 12).

How to calculate the independent *t*-test

A make-believe example relating to scores on a test performed after conditions A and B of no sleep or eight hours' sleep last night will be used to demonstrate how to calculate the test.

- Construct an appropriate table for the calculation of an independent *t*-test.

Participant	Scores on test for condition A (no sleep)	A scores²	Participant	Scores on test for condition B (sleep)	B scores²
1	3	9	8	6	36
2	5	25	9	5	25
3	2	4	10	7	49
4	4	16	11	8	64
5	2	4	12	9	81
6	6	36	13	4	16
7	7	49	14	7	49
			15	8	64
			16	9	81
			17	7	49

Table 5.13 Table for the calculation of an independent *t*-test

1. **A:** add all A scores together (no sleep)
   = 29

2. **A:** divide sum of A scores by number of participants in condition A (N_A)
   = 29 ÷ 7
   = 4.14

3. **A:** square each of the A scores (see Table 5.13)

4. **A:** add the squares of the A scores together
   = 143

5. **A:** square the total of all A scores added together
   = 29²
   = 841

6. **A:** divide the total of all A scores added together squared by the number of participants in condition A
   = 841 ÷ 7
   = 120.1

7. **A:** subtract 120.1 from the total of the squares of the A scores added together
   = 143 − 120.1
   = 22.9

8. Repeat steps 1–7 for the B scores (as steps 9–15)

9. **B:** 70

10. **B:** (N_B)
    = 70 ÷ 10
    = 7

11. **B:** (see Table 5.13)

12 B: 514

13 B:
= 70 × 70
= 4900

14 B:
= 4900 ÷ 10
= 490

15 B:
= 514 − 490
= 24

16 Add the scores from steps 7 and 15 together
= 22.9 + 24
= 46.9

17 Divide the result of step 16 by $N_A - 1$ added to $N_B - 1$
= 46.9 ÷ 6 + 9
= 46.9 ÷ 15
= 3.13

18 Find the reciprocal of N_A and N_B and add them together
$= \frac{1}{7} + \frac{1}{10}$
= 0.1429 + 0.1
= 0.2429

19 Multiply result of step 17 by result of step 18
= 3.13 × 0.2429
= 0.76

20 Find the square root of result of step 19
= √0.76
= 0.872

21 Take result of step 10 from result of step 2
= 4.14 − 7
= −2.86

22 Divide result of step 21 by result of step 20 to find t
= −2.86 ÷ 0.872
= −3.28

- Find the cv from an appropriate critical value table – this will be dependent on whether you have a one- or two-tailed hypothesis (in this case it is two-tailed/non-directional), the level of significance used (in this case 0.05) and the number of degrees of freedom ($d.f.$), which can be calculated from $d.f. = N_A + N_B - 2$ (which in this case = 7 + 10 − 2 = 15).

- If t is equal to or greater than the cv (which in this case is 2.131), there is a significant difference and the null hypothesis can be rejected. (Remember: whether a t-value is negative or positive is ignored.)

Level of significance for a one-tailed (directional) hypothesis			
d.f.	0.1	0.05	0.025
Level of significance for a two-tailed (non-directional) hypothesis			
d.f.	0.2	0.1	0.05
1	2.0	6.314	12.706
2	1.895	2.92	4.303
3	1.644	2.353	3.182
4	1.533	2.132	2.776
5	1.487	2.015	2.571
6	1.446	1.943	2.447
7	1.41	1.895	2.365
8	1.4	1.860	2.306
9	1.389	1.833	2.262
10	1.376	1.812	2.228
11	1.368	1.796	2.201
12	1.364	1.782	2.179
13	1.358	1.771	2.16
14	1.355	1.761	2.145
15	1.349	1.753	2.131
16	1.343	1.746	2.12
17	1.338	1.74	2.110
18	1.336	1.734	2.101
19	1.334	1.729	2.093
20	1.332	1.724	2.086
21	1.328	1.721	2.08
22	1.327	1.717	2.074
23	1.325	1.714	2.069
24	1.323	1.711	2.064
25	1.321	1.708	2.06
26	1.318	1.706	2.056
27	1.316	1.703	2.052
28	1.314	1.701	2.048
29	1.312	1.699	2.045
30	1.31	1.697	2.042

Table 5.14 Critical value table for the *t*-test (independent and related *t*-tests)

To be significant, *t* should be equal to or greater than the table value.

Degrees of freedom (*d.f.*) for a related *t*-test = $N - 1$.

Degrees of freedom for an independent *t*-test = $N_1 + N_2 - 2$.

The repeated t-test

Criteria for choice

The repeated *t*-test is used when a repeated design has been used and the data is of interval/ratio level.

■ Rationale of the test

The test compares the size of the differences in the mean scores of two sets of data drawn from related sources (not independent sources) to see if they differ significantly from each other. For example, seeing if the score on a test done by participants after meditating differs significantly from those doing the test without previously meditating.

■ How to calculate the repeated *t*-test

A make-believe example relating to scores on a test performed after meditating (condition A) and without previously meditating (condition B) will be used to demonstrate how to calculate the test.

■ Construct an appropriate table for calculation of a repeated *t*-test.

Participant	Condition A: test scores after meditation	Condition B: test scores without meditation	d: sum of differences between pairs of scores	d^2: squares of sum of differences between pairs of scores
1	3	6	3	9
2	8	14	6	36
3	4	8	4	16
4	6	4	−2	4
5	9	16	7	49
6	2	7	5	25
7	12	19	7	49

Table 5.15 Table for the calculation of a repeated t-test

1. Calculate the difference between each pair of scores (B − A) and place into table

2. Add all the differences between pairs of scores together
   = 30

3. Divide the result from step 2 by the number of pairs of scores (N)
   = 30 ÷ 7
   = 4.29

4. Square the differences between pairs of scores and add all the squares together
   = 188

5. Square the result from step 2 and divide this number by N (the number of pairs of scores)
   = 30 × 30 ÷ 7
   = 900 ÷ 7
   = 128.57

6. Subtract the result of step 5 from the result of step 4
   = 188 − 128.57
   = 59.43

7. Divide the result from step 6 by $N(N − 1)$
   = 59.43 ÷ 42
   = 1.41

8. Find the square root of the result from step 7
   = $\sqrt{1.41}$
   = 1.19

9 Find *t* by dividing the result from step 3 by the result from step 8
   = 4.29 ÷ 1.19
   = 3.61

   - Find the *cv* from an appropriate critical value table – this will be dependent on whether you have a one- or two-tailed hypothesis (in this case it is two-tailed/non-directional), the level of significance used (in this case 0.05) and the number of degrees of freedom (*d.f.*), which can be calculated from *d.f.* = $N - 1$, (which in this case = $7 - 1 = 6$).

   - If *t* is equal to or greater than the *cv* (which in this case is 2.45), there is a significant difference and the null hypothesis can be rejected. (Remember: whether a *t*-value is negative or positive is ignored.)

Section 3: Carrying out the

Planning
It is important to carefully plan your experimental study, to make sure that you cover all of the requirements for the internal assessment. You need to think about how your group will work, how to choose an area or topic for your study, timings, authenticity and how you will actually carry out the study on the day.

Writing the research report
Writing the report is the most important part of the process, as this is where you will share and analyse your findings. Your report should communicate the following:
- What was done
- Why it was done
- What was found
- What it means.

internal assessment

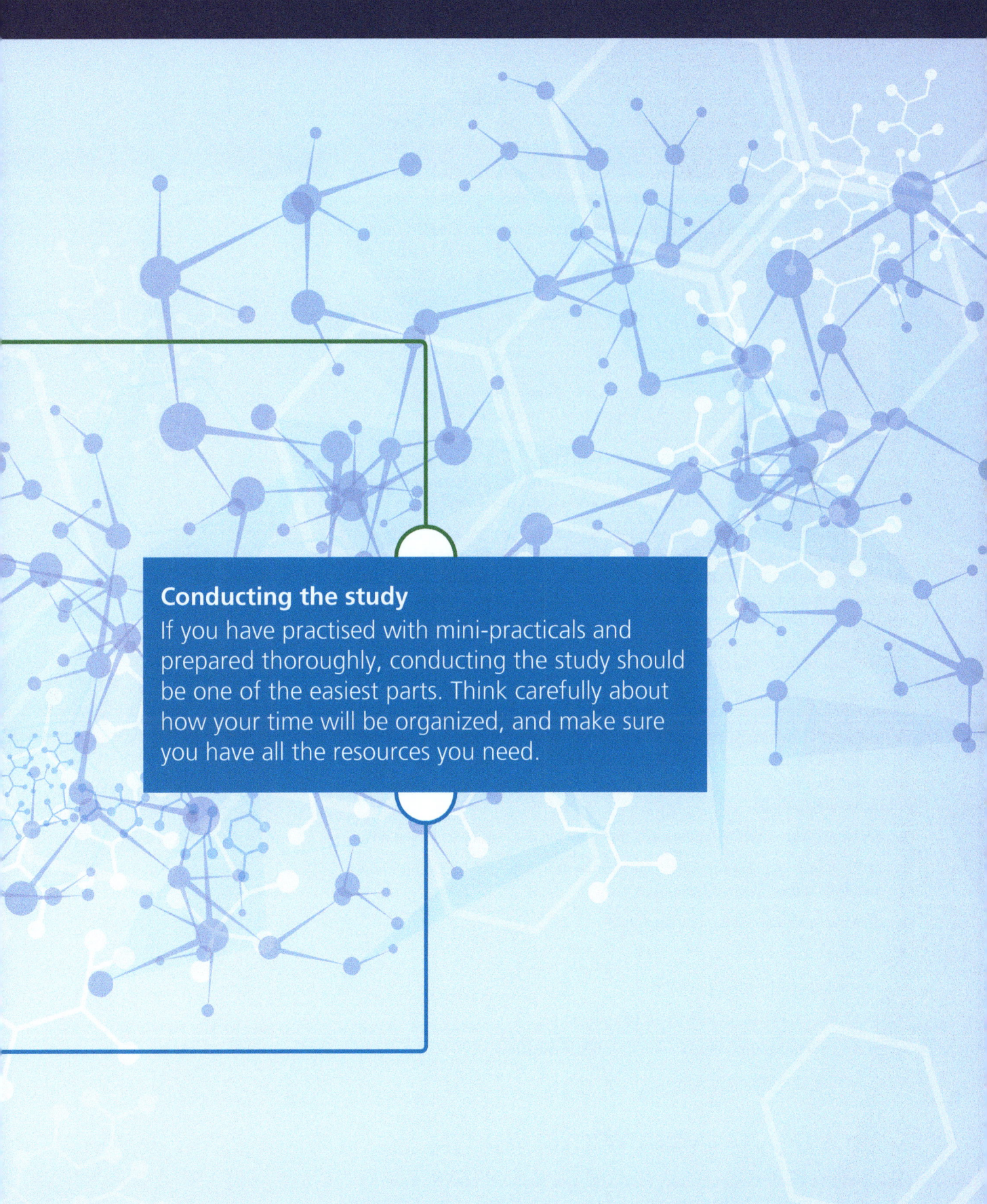

Conducting the study
If you have practised with mini-practicals and prepared thoroughly, conducting the study should be one of the easiest parts. Think carefully about how your time will be organized, and make sure you have all the resources you need.

6 Planning your experimental study

Having familiarized yourselves with the IB's requirements for the internal assessment, how it will be assessed and the elements of research methods that relate to the undertaking of experimental research, as well as hopefully having had a go at some practice mini-practicals, including the usage of relevant inferential statistical tests, let us have a look now at how to actually go about undertaking the study.

This section will take you, step-by-step, through the planning and carrying out of your experiment, with reference to a worked example.

On page 76 you will find a 'tick-list' that details the requirements for planning, carrying out and writing up a research project. You may find this of use when you come to conduct your actual study, with the idea being that you 'tick off' each requirement as it is accomplished.

Group formation

The IB requires that for the experimental study students work in a group of between two and four individuals. The important factor here is to team up with people that you know you can work well with and will not let you down in terms of getting tasks done to deadline. It does not necessarily follow that forming a group with friends will fulfil this purpose. Indeed, friendship groups may spend too much time doing sociable things rather than working on the assessment.

It is also a good idea to have one person in the team who is recognized as the leader, someone who will allocate tasks to different group members and ensure they get done to an agreed timescale. Each member of the group should be given set responsibilities, for example deciding in advance who will provide any necessary materials that are needed for the study. One person will probably have to act as the main researcher in terms of speaking to and directing the participants. This needs to be someone who can speak clearly and who is not nervous about undertaking such a role.

So, once you have agreed who will be in your group and decided who will be in charge, draw up a list of all the tasks that will need to be done in the undertaking of the study. Then, decide who will be responsible for each of these tasks and by what timescale they will be completed. It should be part of the group leader's role to oversee that this is done satisfactorily. The types of tasks that will need to be fulfilled could include:

- deciding on group roles, for example, group leader, data collector and so on
- making decisions about provision of experimental materials, including stimulus materials, data collection sheets and so on
- drawing up of standardized instructions
- creating consent forms
- drawing up a debriefing statement
- creating a data table (to insert your raw data into)
- finding a suitable time and location to conduct the study
- collecting a sample of participants.

Choosing an experimental study

The IB allows a wide range of choice as to what is actually permissible as an experimental study, though reference should be made to the types of independent variables (IVs) not allowed by the IB, for example IVs based on pre-existing characteristics of participants (see page 6). Ultimately, guidance as to what is and isn't allowable should be sought from your teacher before any firm decisions are made about what specifically you are going to study. The experimental study can be based upon any psychological topic of your choice, not necessarily ones on the IB psychology syllabus; in other words, it is an opportunity to explore an area of psychology that interests you.

The basic requirements are that the study:

- *is based on a theory/model/study that has appeared in a peer-reviewed journal* – the theory/model/study your study is based upon must have been published in an officially recognized magazine of scientific studies after passing scrutiny (inspection) by a recognized body of experts
- *is ethical to carry out* – your study must meet the ethical requirements expected for psychological research
- *is practical to carry out* – your study must not pose difficulties in carrying it out, such as requiring extended time periods to perform, requiring materials that are difficult to obtain and so on
- *is based on the experimental method* – your study must not be a correlational study, observational study, self-report, case study and so on
- *has only one independent variable* – you can only manipulate (control) one variable. There may, however, be several conditions of this IV, which will probably be dependent on the number of conditions in the original study that the research is based on. If the original study had several conditions of an IV, this can be replicated in the experimental study, or you could simplify it down to just two conditions.

The dependent variable (DV) does not need to exactly match that within the original study, as long as the link between the study and the experiment being undertaken remains clear and can be justified. For example, if the original study had conditions using specific types of music/songs, you could use other types of music/songs.

You are also allowed to alter the methodology of the study, if it would better suit the context in which you will be working. For example:

- changing the type of participants to school students if it would not be feasible to find non-students
- changing the number of participants if the original study had numbers of participants that would be difficult to replicate
- changing the experimental design, for instance if the original study used a matched participants design and matching would be difficult within a school context.

Once the group has decided on what experimental study to carry out, including what the IV will be, and has identified the original theory/model/study that it will be based upon, this should be submitted to your teacher in the form of a proposal for them to agree to. Once permission has been given by a teacher, you may begin to plan and undertake the study.

Time allowed

The IB does not define a specific time frame in which the experimental study must be performed. There are, however, a recommended number of teaching hours that should be dedicated to the study: your teacher will be aware of these and will make decisions on your behalf on how to use them.

The IB recommends that time is allocated:

- for teachers to explain the requirements of the internal assessment task
- to review the ethical guidelines for the study
- to work on the internal assessment component and ask questions

- for collaboration in groups to occur
- for teachers to consult with groups (and the individuals within them)
- for teachers to review and monitor progress and check the authenticity of your work (that the work is your own).

It is advised that work on the study will not commence until you have reached a level of knowledge and understanding of psychology that would permit you to be able to undertake research. Your teacher will make a decision as to when this level has been reached.

Ultimately, your teacher will set you a deadline for the research report to be completed and handed in, and you must meet this deadline in order for the work to be assessed and moderated. Your teacher may also set an earlier deadline for a first draft of the research report to be handed in, as the IB permits your teacher to give feedback on one initial draft of the research report, after which you make changes before handing in the final version.

Authenticity

It is important that the work you present is your own (other than that permitted from the results of group collaboration). Any form of *plagiarism* (taking someone else's work or ideas and passing them off as your own) is not permitted. This includes copying of material from books, the internet and other students' work. Authenticity of final drafts will be subjected to scrutiny by teachers and moderators appointed by the board, using means such as comparing the style of writing with other work known to be that of the student, and analysis by web-based plagiarism detection tools, such as www.turnitin.com.

> **Worked example**
>
> As a means of making clear what will be required in the planning, undertaking and writing up of an experimental study, a make-believe example will be used as illustration. The example that will be used is an experiment based upon Jenness (1932) into social facilitation.
>
> *This particular experiment, performed as a study of social facilitation by Jenness, is ethically sound, as it does not involve deceit or harm. However, other studies of social influence, such as many studies of conformity and obedience, tend to have unethical elements to them and so would not be permissible as experimental studies for the internal assessment.*
>
> *The study that is featured here is used as an example of how a study would be conducted; it is not done so with the intentions of students copying it in any way.*
>
> Participants individually estimated the number of jelly beans in a jar (a task that was difficult to judge) before and after discussing it in a group and arriving at a group estimate. It was found that participants' second individual estimate was closer to the group norm than their first individual estimate. This supported the idea that people look to others for guidance as how to behave in uncertain situations due to a desire to be correct. The make-believe variation of this will be one where participants have to estimate the number of freckles on a boy's arm before and after discussing it in a group.

Making preparations

What preparations have to be made prior to carrying out a study vary with the nature of the specific study, but some common preparatory tasks are as follows:

1. *Standardized instructions* – a form of control, as well as a means of gaining informed consent from participants, standardized instructions are presented verbally or in written form to all participants and explain the purpose of

the study and exactly what participants will be required to do during it. Participants should be thanked for their interest, given an opportunity to ask questions and reminded that they are under no obligation to take part and may leave at any time they wish. The prime considerations are that standardized instructions are written clearly and do not deceive or misinform the participants in any way.

> **Expert tip**
>
> A copy of the standardized instructions will go in the appendices section of the research report.

Worked example

Exemplar standardized instructions for freckles-on-an-arm study

"Thank you for agreeing to take part in this experiment, which forms part of our IB psychology course; you are under no obligation to complete it and you may leave at any time you wish.

You will be asked to estimate the number of freckles on a boy's arm on several occasions. While doing this, you must not talk to anyone or communicate your estimates to anyone unless you are specifically asked to. Is that clear? Are there any questions?

Let us begin."

2 *Consent forms* – once standardized instructions have been delivered to participants, and as long as they contain sufficient details to allow participants to make a considered decision as to whether they wish to take part in the study, informed consent can be given. This should be recorded on an informed consent form that a participant would sign.

> **Expert tip**
>
> A copy of a blank informed consent form will go in the appendices section of the research report. It should be blank, as participants need to remain anonymous to meet ethical requirements.

Worked example

Exemplar informed consent form for freckles-on-an-arm study

"This experiment is part of our IB psychology course. You are under no obligation to participate and, even if you do consent, you can leave the experiment at any time you wish. If you have understood the standardized instructions and are happy to participate, can you please print and sign your name below."

Name: **Signature:**

3 *Debriefing statement* – presented to participants at the end of a study, a debriefing statement again thanks participants for their help, fully explains the purpose of the study and gives them an opportunity to ask questions about their experience. Results should be shared with participants and any justified deception explained at this point, with the right to withdraw again stated. The debriefing statement should help ensure that participants are not stressed in any way from their experience of taking part in the study.

> **Expert tip**
>
> A copy of the debriefing statement will be placed in the appendices section of your research report.

Worked example

Exemplar debriefing statement for freckles-on-an-arm study

"Thank you again for having helped us with our IB psychology research project. The experiment you have just participated in concerned a type of social influence called social facilitation, which is known as the 'audience effect' and concerns whether people are influenced by the presence of others. The number of freckles on the boy's arm wasn't easy to work out, so we were predicting that participants would look to others who were present for guidance about what the answer should be. If this is true, then the second individual estimates should generally be closer to the group estimate than the first individual estimates, which initial inspection of the results seems to suggest is what happened.

Are there any questions?

Once again, thank you."

4. *Data recording sheet* – as your study will generate data (as a measurement of your DV), you will need to record this data as it is generated (at least one of the group may need to be appointed the task of recording/collecting data). A data recording sheet will need to be designed for the specific requirements of your study.

> **Expert tip**
>
> A completed copy of the data recording sheet (with the data from the study entered on it) will be placed in the appendices of your research report – (a data recording sheet is NOT a results table).

Worked example

Exemplar data recording sheet for freckles-on-an-arm study

(for an example where 21 participants are put into three groups of five participants and one group of six participants)

Participant number	First individual estimate (A)	Distance from group estimate (A)	Group estimate	Distance from group estimate (B)	Second individual estimate (B)
1					
2					
3					
4					
5					
6					
7					
8					
9					
10					
11					
12					
13					
14					
15					
16					
17					
18					
19					
20					
21					

Table 6.1 Exemplar data recording sheet

5. *Materials* – most experimental studies will require some form of stimulus materials, as well as other materials for the smooth conducting of the study. These should be listed and obtained/produced before the start of the study.

> **Expert tip**
>
> Your materials should be listed within the methodology section of your research report.

Worked example

Exemplar materials for freckles-on-an-arm study:

- One boy with freckled arm
- 21 'First individual estimate' cards for before being in a group (numbered 1–21)
- 21 'Second individual estimate' cards for after being in a group (numbered 1–21)
- 4 'Group estimate' cards, labelled according to the participants in each group (Participants 1–5, Participants 6–10, Participants 11–15, Participants 16–21).

6 *Choosing a laboratory* – the term laboratory conjures up images of white-coated scientists and bubbling test-tubes, but for the purpose of a psychology experiment, a laboratory simply means a controlled testing environment. It will be the place where your participants are tested under controlled conditions. In order to effectively achieve this, it is advised that you choose somewhere that has little risk of distractions. Therefore, it should be a relatively quiet place, without windows if possible, where participants will feel comfortable, but not distracted. Your teacher may be able to suggest/arrange somewhere suitable within your school/college, but there is no stipulation that your laboratory has to be on school/college premises; anywhere that meets the requirements of being a safe, controllable and accessible venue will be sufficient.

7 *Conducting a pilot study* – however well you think you've designed your study and prepared for all eventualities, you probably haven't! A pilot study is a small-scale pre-study; in other words, it is a 'trial run' of your assessed experimental study. You could possibly use a few members of another psychology group to act as participants for your pilot study (and maybe return the favour for them). A pilot study allows you to do the following:

- *See if there's anything worth investigating* – there is probably no point conducting a study if the pilot study suggests there is no chance of finding anything of interest. For example, it would be pointless to conduct an experiment into gender differences in short-term memory capacity – there aren't any.

- *Identify and remedy errors in the methodology* – by conducting a pilot study, you may be able to identify areas in your design methodology or analysis, for example faults in the procedure, that could be improved.

- *Give participants a chance to give feedback on the experience* – participants in a pilot study see the study from a different perspective that may allow them to provide useful feedback that allows you to make useful changes. For example, they might report that the standardized instructions are unclear and need some re-writing.

> **Expert tip**
>
> Details about your pilot study can be reported in the methodology section of your research report.

8 *Obtaining a sample of participants* – as researchers do not generally have the time or resources to test whole target populations (groups of people whom conclusions about experimental findings are directed at), it is customary to test instead a sample (part) of the target population that is *representative* (closely matches the characteristics of the target population). The IB syllabus refers to several sampling methods, but focus here will be on those sampling methods you are most likely to use (with an explanation given of each, plus an examination of their strengths and weaknesses), as these could feature in the discussion part of your research report.

If you are using an independent groups design, then a sample of about 20 participants is regarded as being acceptable for an appropriate inferential statistical test to be able to find a significant difference, if one exists. For a repeated measures design (as each participant generates two pieces of data), about 10 participants would be acceptable.

■ Random sampling

Selection occurs without bias, which is achieved by each member of a population having an equal chance of being chosen. One way to do this is to place all names from the target population in a container and draw out the required sample number. Computer programs are also used to generate random lists.

■ Strengths

- *Unbiased selection* – as there is no prejudice in selection, it increases the chances of getting a representative sample.

- *Generalisation* – as the sample should be fairly representative, results will be generalizable (said to be true of) the target population.

Weaknesses

- *Impractical* – random sampling is difficult to achieve, as it is often difficult to get full details of a target population and not all members may be available or wish to take part. Indeed, it may be a certain 'type' from a target population that doesn't wish to take part, making the findings unrepresentative.
- *Not representative* – unbiased selection does not guarantee an unbiased sample. For example, all females could be randomly selected, making the sample unrepresentative and thus the results not generalizable.

Opportunity sampling

Selection occurs of participants who are available and willing to take part, for example asking people in the street who are passing.

Strengths

- *Ease of formation* – opportunity samples are relatively easy to create, as they use people who are readily available.

Weaknesses

- *Unrepresentative* – an opportunity sample is likely to be biased by excluding certain types of participants. Therefore, because it would be unrepresentative, findings could not be generalised to the target population. For instance, an opportunity sample collected in town during the day on a weekday would not include those at work or college.
- *Self-selection* – participants have the option to decline to take part and the sampling technique thus turns into a self-selected sample.

Volunteer (self-selected) sampling

Selection occurs of people who offer themselves as participants, usually in response to an advertisement/poster to take part.

Strengths

- *Ease of formation* – creation of a self-selected sample needs little effort from the researchers (other than producing an advert/poster), as participants volunteer themselves.
- *Less chance of the 'screw you' phenomenon* – as participants are keen to take part, there will be less chance of them deliberately trying to sabotage the study.

Weaknesses

- *Unrepresentative* – the sample may be biased, as volunteers tend to be a certain 'type' of person. Therefore, it would be unrepresentative, making results not generalizable to a target population.
- *Demand characteristics* – volunteers are keen to please, increasing the chances of demand characteristics. For example, participants may give the answer they think is required.

> **Expert tip**
>
> As obtaining a truly random sample is very difficult to achieve, for reasons already explained, it is more likely your experimental study will use either an opportunity or self-selected (volunteer) sample. There are strengths and weaknesses to using both of these and a choice will ultimately need to be made.
>
> One important measure to consider with opportunity samples is to try and avoid selecting people who are known to you, for example friends and family; due to their relationships with you, there will be an increased chance of demand characteristics and thus unrepresentative findings.
>
> Random sampling should be used within the study to allocate without bias (if you are using an independent groups design) which participants in your sample will do which conditions of your study.

7 Conducting the study

Compared to the planning and writing up of the experimental study, the actual carrying out of it is probably the easiest part. If you have prepared thoroughly for the study, then there is no reason why it should not go smoothly.

It is important, though, that you adequately timetable your study in terms of how long it will take to process participants and make sure everyone who is needed is available at the time(s) you intend to do the study. Depending on the specific study, you will either be testing participants individually, in groups or as individuals in one large group. For instance, in the make-believe freckles-on-an-arm study, participants could either be processed in small groups (as a group estimate would need to be formed) or as one large group of individuals, with divisions into smaller groups during the study.

Once your participants have arrived at the laboratory at the designated time (either individually or as a group), you will need to:

- deliver the standardized instructions
- answer any initial queries about the study
- collect signed informed consent forms
- remind participants of their right to withdraw
- conduct the study
- collect the data generated
- deliver the debriefing statement
- answer any questions
- thank your participants and dismiss them.

Analysing the data

Data will need to be analysed using:

1. descriptive statistics (see page 37)
2. inferential statistics (see page 39).

8 Writing the research report

In psychology, there is a convention that research studies should be written up in a certain way. This is so that results can be checked for validity (accuracy) by the study being replicated (repeated exactly) by other researchers. A good way to explain this process is to think of the research report as like a recipe for a cake. If a recipe is written so that all the ingredients are listed and the procedure is clearly explained in a step-by-step nature, then exactly the same cake should be produced every time.

The basic requirements of a research report are to communicate:

- what was done
- why it was done
- what was found
- what it means.

Although the planning and carrying out of the experimental study are important in themselves (and indeed the writing of an effective research report would not be possible without them being well executed), the research report is the most important part of the process, as it is the only part for which marks are awarded.

Let us therefore go through the writing up of a research report, section by section, with reference to the make-believe freckles-on-an-arm study, with some additional focus on the awarding of marks for the IB internal assessment.

Title page

The title page needs to include the following:

- A title that clearly describes the study, for example:

    A *laboratory experiment of social facilitation using a Jenness-type task*

- Your IB candidate code, for example, ZYX321
- IB candidate code for all group members
- Date, month and year of submission
- Number of words (*the report, in total, should be between 1,800 and 2,200 words – not inclusive of graphs, tables, references and appendices*).

The introduction component

Six marks are available for this section, which are awarded from level descriptors (see page 8). Following the conventional way to write a research report, this will be divided into the sub-sections of abstract, introduction, and aims and hypotheses.

The abstract (summary)

- The abstract is a summary of your **aim**, your **hypothesis**, your **methodology**, your **results** and your **conclusion**.
- The abstract should also contain **where you got the idea from** (previous research).
- The abstract should not include any **details** or **evaluation**.

For example:

The aim of this experiment, based on Jenness (1932), was to see if people are socially facilitated by the presence of others in uncertain situations. Using a repeated measures design, an opportunity sample of 21 office workers saw a boy's arm and made an individual estimate of how many freckles were on it. They then discussed it in groups and came up with a group estimate. They then saw the arm again and made a second individual estimate. It was hypothesised that the second individual estimate would be closer to the group estimate than their first individual estimate. The results confirmed this as true. It was concluded that people are influenced by others present in uncertain situations.

The introduction

The introduction details and explains the particular topic area you are researching, including the theory/model and/or study your research is based upon. The idea is that your aims and hypotheses will be based upon what is expected to happen according to previous research and theory. This link should be clearly explained.

A 'funnel' approach is a useful way of composing the introduction, where you firstly introduce the general topic area then narrow down the focus onto the specific theory and/or study you are investigating.

For example:

This experiment investigates social influence – how people affect each other. The particular aspect of social influence being studied is social facilitation. Known as the 'audience effect', this involves the extent to which people are affected by the presence of others in social situations. The degree of effect is influenced by the size and type of the audience and by the type and complexity of the social situation. Being influenced by others can facilitate an evolutionary survival value, as guidance from others present can provide information about how to behave in potentially dangerous situations (and thus be a life-saver). Therefore, it can be seen how social facilitation may have evolved, as those with the genes to be influenced by others to avoid risky situations would have survived to sexual maturity and reproduced. Consequently, over time, by the process of natural selection, the behaviour would become more widespread. This might also explain why the behaviour is unconscious and does not need to be taught, as it is coded into our genes.

Jenness' (1932) experiment aimed to see if participants were socially facilitated by a group of people in an ambiguous situation. He asked participants to individually estimate the number of jellybeans in a jar, which was a difficult task to achieve. Then, in small groups, he asked them to agree upon a group estimate. Finally, he asked them to make another individual estimate. He found that the second estimate converged towards the group estimate, suggesting that people's behaviour is facilitated by the presence of others in uncertain situations. This was a phenomenon that Jenness referred to as a 'typicality of effect'.

The experiment being conducted here uses a variation of Jenness's procedure, so a similar result should be expected.

The aims and hypotheses

The aims and hypotheses should emerge from (be linked to) the material discussed in your introduction.

- **The aim** – a statement that conveys the purpose of the experimental study; it outlines what specifically is being investigated. For example:

    To assess whether people are affected by social facilitation in uncertain situations, by investigating whether people's individual estimates of freckles on a male's arm move closer to a group estimate discussion.

- **The hypotheses** – predictions of the results that might occur in the study.

- You will need two hypotheses: an experimental hypothesis (that predicts a significant difference between your two conditions of the IV) and a null hypothesis (that predicts no significant difference between your two conditions of the IV).
- Your experimental hypothesis should be *directional* (one-tailed), if previous research, e.g. Jenness (1932), gives an indication of which direction the results should lie in.
- Your hypotheses are probably best expressed (in terms of maximizing your marks according to the IB assessment criteria) by including operationalized (clearly defined) references to both the IV (in this example the first individual estimate made before the group estimate and the second individual estimate made after the group estimate) and the DV (in this example the distance of the individual estimates from the group estimate). For example:

  Experimental (one-tailed)

  That participants' second individual estimates of the number of freckles on a male's arm will be closer to a group estimate than their first individual estimates.

  Null

  That participants' second individual estimates of the number of freckles on a male's arm will be no closer to a group estimate than their first individual estimates.

The exploration component

Four marks are available for this section, which are awarded from level descriptors (see page 8). Following the conventional way to write a research report, this will involve the design and methodology sub-section.

Design and methodology

- This sub-section explains details of the design and methodology of your experimental report and can be sub-divided into relevant parts with subtitles.
- **Design** – explains details of the design, but without a need for evaluation (there is no need to explain strengths and weaknesses). The independent variable (IV) and the dependent variable (DV) should be identified and clearly operationalized (defined in terms of the experiment). For example:

  The experimental method was used, with the type of experiment being a laboratory experiment, taking place under controlled conditions. The experimental design used was the repeated measures design, as each participant performed in both conditions of the independent variable (IV). It was not possible to counterbalance for order effects, as the order of presentation of the two conditions of the IV were fixed. The independent variable, manipulated by the researchers, was whether an individual estimate was made before or after a group estimate was made. The dependent variable (DV), a measurement of the effect of the IV, was the distance of individual estimates from a group estimate.

- **Sampling** – explains the sampling method used (the means by which participants were chosen for the study). The following details about participants should be given:
  1. Total number of participants
  2. Number of males and females
  3. Age range of participants
  4. Background details of participants.
     For example:
     Opportunity sampling was used. Participants who were available and willing to take part were utilized, by asking individual office workers at a local company if they wished to participate. 21 participants were used in total; 10 were male and 11 were female. Their ages ranged between 19 and 62.

- **Controls** – the means by which potential extraneous variables were controlled should be explained here. Materials placed in appendices should be referenced here. For example:
  - ☐ Controlled conditions were established to minimize the possibility of variables other than the IV having an effect on the DV.
  - ☐ **Participant controls**
    All participants did all conditions of the experiment, and therefore there were no participant variables between the conditions.
  - ☐ **Situational controls**
    All participants were tested in a quiet stockroom in the office premises, so there was minimal noise or other distraction, and the room remained at a moderate, stable temperature throughout.
  - ☐ **Experimental controls**
    All participants were subjected to the same procedure in the same way, being shown the male's freckled arm for the same amount of time. Participants sat around a table so that viewing conditions of the freckled arm were similar. Aside from discussion in small groups, participants were not allowed to talk during the study to minimize the risk of demand characteristics (by others' comments influencing individual behaviour). Identical-looking (other than the participant numbers on them) scorecards were used to record estimates and these were completed in an identical fashion.

- **Procedure** – details of the procedure used are explained in a step-by-step nature, with any materials placed in the appendices referenced here.
  For example:
  - ☐ A small-scale pilot study conducted before the main study identified that parts of the standardized instructions were a little vague, so these were subsequently made clearer. It was also reported at this stage that the lead researcher spoke too quickly for participants to follow, so she thereafter slowed down speed of delivery.
  - ☐ Participants were informed of the aims of the study and reminded of their right to withdraw.
  - ☐ Informed consent forms were signed and collected in.
  - ☐ Each participant was numbered from 1 to 21 by random selection (numbers were drawn from a container) and seated around a large table.
  - ☐ Participants were shown the boy's freckled arm for 5 seconds and asked to record on 'First individual estimate' cards (see appendices) their estimate of the number of freckles on his arm. Participants were reminded to remain silent and not communicate their estimates to other participants.
  - ☐ Scorecards were collected in and scores placed onto the data recording sheet (see appendices).
  - ☐ Participants were divided into three groups of five participants and one group of six participants (1–5, 6–10, 11–15, 16–21) and asked to arrive at a group estimate. Four small tables were used for this purpose so that other groups could not hear their discussions. Participants were again reminded not to communicate their group estimates in any way to other groups. Group estimates were recorded on 'Group estimate' cards by one member of each group (see appendices).
  - ☐ Group estimate cards were collected in and scores placed onto the data recording sheet (see appendices).
  - ☐ Participants then returned to their original positions and were again shown the boy's freckled arm for 5 seconds and asked to record, on 'Second individual estimate' cards (see appendices), their estimate of the number of freckles on his arm. They were once more reminded to remain silent and not communicate their estimates to other participants.

- Scorecards were collected and scores placed onto the data recording sheet (see appendices).
- Participants were then thanked for their cooperation and debriefed fully about the investigation, with an opportunity given to ask any questions they had.

■ **Ethical considerations** – although the IB assessment criteria do not mention ethical guidelines in the awarding of marks, their guidance notes do state that ethical guidelines should be adhered to in the reporting of the experimental study. So ethical issues relevant to the study should be identified here, with an explanation given as to how they were dealt with. For example:

- *Informed consent was gained by giving participants, all of whom were over 16 years of age, sufficient details of the study so that they could make an informed decision as to whether they wished to take part. Informed consent forms were signed and collected from all participants (see appendices). Participants were explicitly told they did not have to complete the study and could leave at any point.*
- *The right to withdraw was emphasized by participants being explicitly told that they were not obliged to take part and could leave at any time.*
- *Deceit was dealt with by participants not being misled in any way about the purpose or procedures of the study.*
- *Protection from harm was dealt with by participants not being put under any stress greater than that experienced in everyday life. Participants were also fully debriefed after the study to reassure them about their individual contributions to the study.*
- *Anonymity was dealt with by participants being referred to throughout the study, including the research report, by numbers and not actual names.*

■ **Materials** – the materials used in the study are identified and explained. For example:

- *21 'First individual estimate' recording cards, numbered 1–21, for recording individual estimates before a group estimate was established*
- *21 'Second individual estimate' recording cards, numbered 1–21, for recording individual estimates after a group estimate was established*
- *4 'Group estimate' recording cards, labelled according to the participants in each group (Participants 1–5, Participants 6–10, Participants 11–15, Participants 16–21), for recording group estimates*
- *1 data collection sheet, for entering individual estimates (before and after forming group estimates) and group estimates*
- *Set of standardized instructions for presentation to participants prior to study, detailing procedures and purpose of study*
- *Debriefing statement for presentation to participants at conclusion of study*
- *1 male with freckled arm, presented during study as stimulus material.*

The analysis component

Six marks are available for this section, which are awarded from level descriptors (see page 9). Following the conventional way to write a research report, this will involve the results sub-section, divided into:

■ descriptive results
■ inferential results.

Tables and graphs do not count towards the final word count. Data collected should be displayed appropriately, with raw data placed in the appendices. Descriptive statistical analysis should show the variability and spread of scores. Inferential statistical analysis should allow conclusions to be drawn about the significance of data in terms of the hypotheses.

■ Descriptive results

Findings here are described in numerical form (in terms of a results table), visual form (in terms of a graph) and verbal form (in terms of a written description of the results). Appropriate reference should be made to measures of central tendency (averages or 'middle' numbers) and measures of dispersion (the spread of scores). For example, see Tables 8.1–8.2 and Figures 8.1–8.2.

	Number	Percentage
Participants whose second individual estimates were closer to the group estimate than their first	17	81%
Participants whose second estimates were further from the group estimate than their first	2	9.5%
Participants whose second estimate was neither closer to nor further from the group estimate	2	9.5%
Total	21	100%

Table 8.1 Table showing number of participants moving towards/away from a group estimate

	Before group estimates were formed	After group estimates were formed
Total difference of individual estimates from group estimates	8350	2890
Mean difference of individual estimates from group estimates	397.6	137.6
Distance between highest and lowest differences of individual estimates from group estimates	1300	600

Table 8.2 Table showing totals, means and ranges of individual differences from group estimates

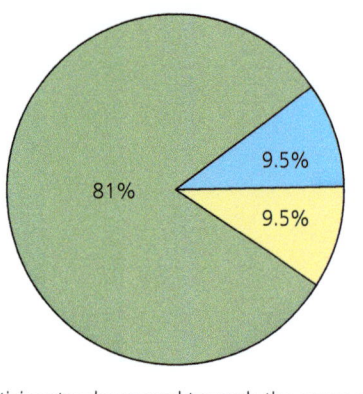

■ % of participants who moved towards the group estimate
□ % of participants who moved away from the group estimate
■ % of participants who didn't change their estimates

Figure 8.1 Pie chart showing percentage of participants moving towards/away from a group estimate

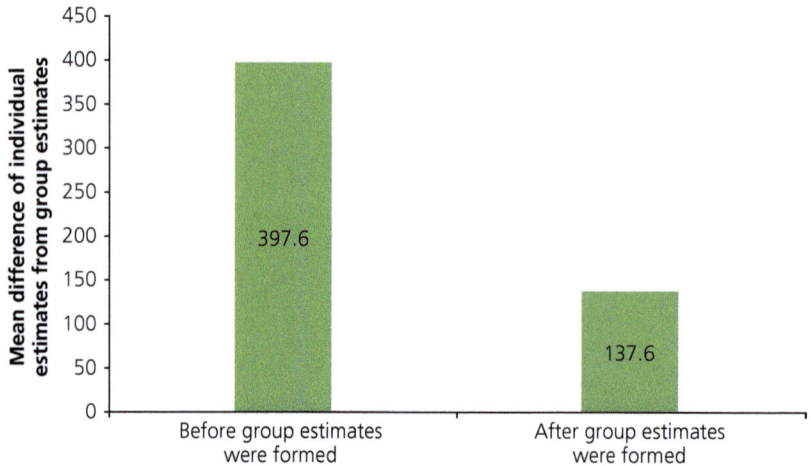

Figure 8.2 Bar chart showing mean differences of individual estimates of freckles on an arm from group estimates

■ Descriptive results

17 out of 21 participants (81%) had an individual estimate formed after group discussion that was closer to the group estimate than their individual estimate formed before group discussion.

2 participants (9.5%) had an individual estimate formed after group discussion that was further from the group estimate than their individual estimate formed before group discussion.

2 participants (9.5%) had an individual estimate formed after group discussion that was neither closer to nor further away from the group estimate than their individual estimate formed before group discussion.

The total difference of individual estimates from group estimates before group estimates were formed was 8350, with a mean difference of 397.6.

The total difference of individual estimates from group estimates after group estimates were formed was 2890, with a mean difference of 137.6.

The range of differences of individual estimates from group estimates before group estimates were formed was 1300.

The range of differences of individual estimates from group estimates after group estimates were formed was 600.

Inferential results

Findings here are subjected to appropriate statistical analysis, with the test used being fully justified in terms of the level of data and experimental design used. The result should be expressed in terms of the hypotheses with reference to the appropriate fully justified critical value. Calculations of the test should be referenced to the appendices section. For example:

The data was subjected to a Wilcoxon signed-matched ranks inferential statistical test, as a difference between two conditions of an IV was being tested for, data was of at least ordinal level and a repeated measures design was used.

After subjecting the data to the tests, a significant difference was found and the null hypothesis rejected.

Component	Value
N	19
T	10
Significance level	0.05
cv for one-tailed hypothesis	53

Table 8.3 Table of results for Wilcoxon signed-matched ranks test

(Calculations for the test can be found in the appendices.)

The evaluation component

Six marks are available for this section, which are awarded from level descriptors (see page 9). Following the conventional way to write a research report, this will involve the discussion sub-section.

Discussion

The discussion provides an evaluation of the study. Although not traditionally divided into formal sub-sections, there are a number of different aspects that can be addressed within the discussion.

- **Results** – it is customary to begin the discussion with an explanation of the results in terms of the hypotheses. For example:

  The majority (17/21) of participants' second individual estimates were closer to the group estimates than their first individual estimates, with total and mean differences of estimates from group estimates backing this up. Coupled with inferential statistical analysis finding a significant difference, it validates the experimental hypothesis. This suggests that people are affected by others present in uncertain situations, as they have a need to be correct which has an evolutionary advantage in increasing survival chances. Because the experiment took place under controlled conditions, causality is suggested. As both male and females were used, the results are generalizable to both genders.

- **Previous research and theory** – results are discussed in terms of theories/models and research outlined in the introduction, especially in terms of whether the findings match those predicted. For example:

  Just as Jenness found that participants were influenced by the presence of others in uncertain situations, this experiment similarly found this to be true, due to social facilitation, where people behave differently when in the presence of others than when alone. Others present may be seen as being more knowledgeable and thus able to communicate guidance as to what would be more effective behaviour in a given situation, therefore producing a 'typicality of effect'.

- **Limitations and modifications** – weaknesses in the methodology used are identified, with suggestions given as to how modifications could lessen these weaknesses so that more effective data, and thus firmer conclusions, could be arrived at. For example:

  The experiment had several limitations. It lacks ecological validity as the task wasn't an everyday one. This could be remedied by using a task more relevant to real life, such as assessing the number of people in a crowd, or the number of books in a library. The use of an opportunity sample presents problems of generalization, as participants tend to be of one 'type'. Using participants from a wider background may have created more representative results. The participants were also known to each other, which may have led to their personal relationships with one another affecting the behaviour. For example, not wanting to disagree with someone of a higher social standing, such as a line manager. This would be remedied by using participants who were unknown to each other.

- **Practical applications and ideas for future research** – although not mentioned in the IB assessment criteria, it is customary to comment on practical applications of the research and ideas for future research that are suggested by the findings. For example:

  The results suggest a practical application. Tasks involving ambiguity and uncertainty could be used when forming groups of individuals in order to draw them together into a cohesive unit.

  An area for future research is to focus on the relationship of participants to each other. Those in this study were known to each other and were part of a social structure; it would be interesting to see if the social facilitation effect was greater when participants were unknown to each other and so other social variables were removed.

- **Conclusion** – it is customary with the discussion to finish with a short, overall concluding statement. For example:

  Overall, it seems that people are socially facilitated by the presence of others in uncertain situations to produce a typicality of effect that may incur an evolutionary survival value.

The references and appendices

No marks are awarded under the IB assessment criteria for inclusion of the references and appendices sub-sections of the research report. However, without them it would not be possible to authenticate references quoted within the study, nor to check the validity of mathematical and statistical calculations. Therefore, it is expected that they will be included in the conventional manner of writing a research report.

References

Full details of references should be listed in a standard format in terms of the books, internet sources and journals that they were sourced from. References and appendices do not count towards the final word count. For example:

Jenness, A. (1932) The role of discussion in changing opinion regarding a matter of fact. *Journal of Abnormal and Social Psychology,* 27(3), 279–296.

Appendices

The appendices contain all materials referenced within the report, including raw data and mathematical and statistical calculations.

For example:

Appendix I: Standardized instructions

Thank you for agreeing to take part in this experiment; you are under no obligation to complete it and you may leave at any time you wish.

You will be asked to estimate the number of freckles on a boy's arm on several occasions. While doing this, you must not talk to anyone or communicate your estimates to anyone unless you are specifically asked to. Is that clear? Are there any questions?

Let us begin.

Appendix II: Informed consent form

This experiment is part of our IB psychology course. You are under no obligation to participate and, even if you do consent, you can leave the experiment at any time you wish. If you have understood the standardized instructions and are happy to participate, can you please print and sign your name below.

Name: **Signature:**

Appendix III: Debriefing statement

Thank you again for having helped us with our IB psychology research project. The experiment you have just participated in concerned a type of social influence called social facilitation, which is known as the 'audience effect' and concerns whether people are influenced by the presence of others. The number of freckles on the boy's arm wasn't easy to work out, so we were predicting that participants would look to others who were present for guidance about what the answer should be. If this is true, then the second individual estimates should generally be closer to the group estimate than the first individual estimates, which initial inspection of the results seems to suggest is what happened.

Are there any questions?

Once again, thank you.

Appendix IV: Data table

Participant number	First individual estimate	Distance of first individual estimate from group estimate	Group estimate	Distance of second individual estimate from group estimate	Second individual estimate
1	200	400	600	300	300
2	500	100	600	100	500
3	700	100	600	0	600
4	800	200	600	100	700
5	550	50	600	0	600
6	1000	100	900	50	950
7	2000	1100	900	100	1000
8	500	400	900	200	700
9	400	500	900	100	800
10	550	350	900	400	500
11	150	1350	1500	500	1000
12	1000	500	1500	100	1400
13	2500	1000	1500	0	1500
14	900	600	1500	0	1500
15	400	1100	1500	600	900
16	500	150	650	150	500
17	600	50	650	0	650
18	700	50	650	100	750
19	800	150	650	50	600
20	700	50	650	30	680
21	600	50	650	10	640

Table 8.4 Data table

Appendix V: Calculations for descriptive statistics

Total sum of differences of first individual estimates from group estimates
= 400 + 100 + 100 + 200 + 50 + 100 + 1100 + 400 + 500 + 350 + 1350 + 500 + 1000 + 600 + 1100 + 150 + 50 + 50 + 150 + 50 + 50
= 8350

Mean sum of differences of first individual estimates from group estimates
= 8350 ÷ 21
= 397.6

Total sum of differences of second individual estimates from group estimates
= 300 + 100 + 0 + 100 + 0 + 50 + 100 + 200 + 100 + 400 + 500 + 100 + 0 + 0 + 600 + 150 + 0 + 100 + 50 + 30 + 10
= 2890

Mean sum of differences of second individual estimates from group estimates
= 2890 ÷ 21
= 137.6

Range of differences of individual estimates from group estimates before group estimates were formed
= 1350 − 50
= 1300

Range of differences of individual estimates from group estimates after group estimates were formed
= 600 − 0
= 600

Appendix VI: Table and calculations for Wilcoxon signed-matched ranks test

Participant	Distance from group estimate A	Distance from group estimate B	Differences between A and B scores	Ranks
1	400	300	−100	9.5
2	100	100	0	Omitted
3	100	0	−100	9.5
4	200	100	−100	9.5
5	50	0	−50	5
6	100	50	−50	5
7	1100	100	−1000	18.5
8	400	200	−200	12
9	500	100	−400	13.5
10	350	400	+50	5
11	1350	500	−850	17
12	500	100	−400	13.5
13	1000	0	−1000	18.5
14	600	0	−600	16
15	1100	600	−500	15
16	150	150	0	Omitted
17	50	0	−50	5
18	50	100	+50	5
19	150	50	−100	9.5
20	50	30	−20	1
21	50	10	−10	2

Table 8.5 Table for Wilcoxon signed-matched ranks test

T = sum of ranks for the less frequent sign
= 5 + 5
= 10

cv with a one-tailed hypothesis, a 0.05 significance level and N (the number of ranked pairs) = 19 is 53.

Comparing T to the cv shows it to be equal to or lower than the cv; therefore there is a significant difference and the null hypothesis can be rejected.

Appendix VII: Supplementary materials

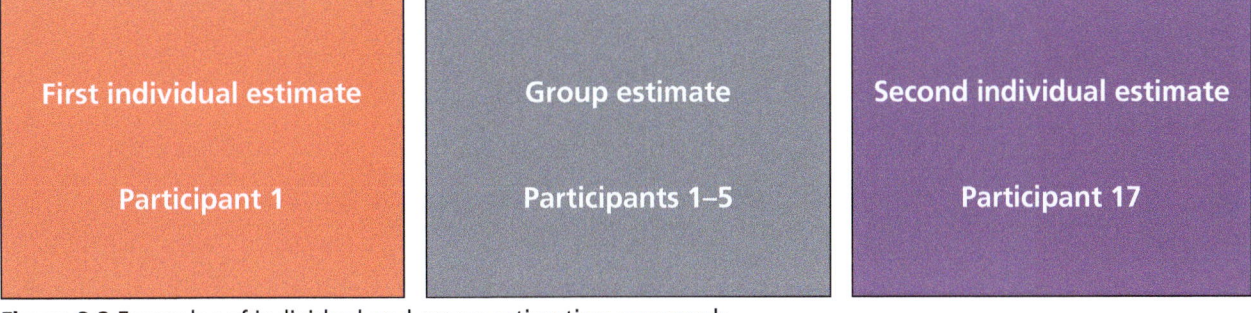

Figure 8.3 Examples of individual and group estimation scorecards

IB Psychology experimental study

'Tick-list' for conducting an experimental study

You may find this experimental study 'tick-list' of use. It details most requirements for planning, carrying out and writing up a research project. It could also easily be adapted for experiments with different requirements.

Team formation

Team organized	

Allocate jobs

Materials	
Composing score/data sheets	
Writing standardized Instructions	
Allocating researcher roles	
Composing debriefing statement	
Data collection	
Composing informed consent form	

Preparation

Standardized instructions complete	
Debriefing statement complete	
Score/data sheets complete	
Materials ready	
Pilot study carried out	
Informed consent form complete	

Carrying out study

Data collected	

Writing up practical

Preparation

Title page	
List of contents	
Abstract	
Introduction	
Aims	
Hypotheses	

Methodology

Design	
Controls	
i) Participant controls	
ii) Situational controls	
iii) Experimental controls	
Procedure & materials	

Presentation of results: *descriptive analysis*

Table	
Graph	
Words	

Presentation of results: *inferential analysis*

Inferential test chosen and justified	
Inferential statistical test completed	

Discussion

Explanation of findings	
Relationship to background research	
Limitations and modifications	
Implications, applications and ideas for future research	

Others

References	
Appendices	

Rewrite

Alterations complete	

Template for mini-practicals

Abstract

Previous related research indicates

Research aims

Hypotheses

Brief description of research method and design

Sampling method and details

IV DV

Ethical considerations	Pilot study indicated

Template for mini-practicals

Results table

Graph

Verbal results summary

Inferential statistical test details

Hypothesis acceptance

Evaluation

Conclusion

Future research idea

References

Abernethy, E.M. (1940) The effect of changed environmental conditions upon the results of college examinations. *Journal of Psychology*, 10, 293–301.

Allport, G. and Postman, L. (1947) *The Psychology of Rumor*. New York: Holt, Rinehart and Winston.

Asch, S. (1956) Studies of independence and conformity: a minority of one against a unanimous majority. *Psychological Monographs: General and Applied*, 70(9), 1–70.

Bickman, L. (1974) The social power of a uniform. *Journal of Applied Social Psychology*, 4(1), 47–61.

Brochet, F. and Dubourdieu, D. (2001) Wine descriptive language supports cognitive specificity of chemical senses. *Brain and Language*. 77(2), 187–196.

Bruner, J.S. and Postman, L. (1947) Tension and tension release as organizing factors in perception. *Journal of Personality*, 15, 300–308.

Costello, E., Compton, S., Keeler, G. and Angold, A. (2003) Relationships between poverty and psychopathology: a natural experiment. *JAMA*, 290(15), 2023–2029.

Herlitz, A., Nilsson, L-G. and Backman, L. (1997) Gender differences in episodic memory. *Memory and Cognition*, 25(6), 801–811.

Heydorn, S., Menne, T. and Johansen, J. D. (2003) Fragrance allergy and hand eczema – a review. *Contact Dermatitis*, 48(2), 59–66.

Jacobs, J. (1887) Experiments in prehension. *Mind*, 12, 75–79.

Jenness, A. (1932) The role of discussion in changing opinion regarding a matter of fact. *Journal of Abnormal and Social Psychology*, 27(3), 279–296.

Lawton, J-M. & Willard, E. (2018) *Psychology for the IB Diploma* (second edition). London: Hodder Education.

Marsh, R. L., Sebrechts, M.M., Hicks, J.L. and Landau, J.D. (1997) Processing strategies and secondary memory in very rapid forgetting. *Memory and Cognition*, 25, 173–181.

Index

A
Abernethy 34–6
Allport 28
analytical skills 4, 5
animal participants 7, 16
Asch 18
assessment criteria 8–9

B
bar charts 23, 26, 30, 37, 70
bias 14
Bickman 16
Brochet and Dubourdieu 33
Bruner 28

C
causality 12, 13
chi-squared test 30–2, 41, 42–4
confounding variables 12–13
consent forms 59
Costello et al. 17

D
data recording sheet 60
debriefing statement 59
deception 7
demand characteristics 13–14, 15, 18, 19, 62
dependent variable (DV) 12
deprivation, studies involving 6
descriptive skills 4, 5
descriptive statistical analysis 37–8, 69–70
double-blind procedure 14

E
ecological validity 23
ethical guidelines 7
evaluative skills 4, 5
exhalation, studies involving 6
experimental design 17–19
experimental method 12
experimental study
  authenticity 58
  choosing 56–7
  conducting 63
  group formation 56
  making preparations 58–62
  sample 61–2
  tick list 76–7
  time allowed 57–8
experimenter variables 13
experiments, types of 15–17
external validity 15
extraneous variables 12–13

F
field experiments 16
frequency polygons 38

G
graphs 37
group formation 56

H
Herlitz et al. 17, 32
Heydorn et al. 19
histograms 38

I
IB requirements 5–7, 56–8
identical twins 19
independent groups design (IGD) 14, 17, 18, 41
independent t-test 41, 48–51
independent variable (IV) 6, 12
inferential statistical tests 39–53, 71
ingestion, studies involving 7
interval/ratio data 40, 41
investigator effects 14

J
Jacobs 20
Jenness 18, 58, 65, 72

L
laboratory experiments 15
line graphs 38

M
Mann-Whitney test 41, 44–6
Marsh et al. 15
matched participants design (MPD) 17, 19
mini-practicals
  Abernethy (1940) 34–6
  Brochet and Dubourdieu (2001) 33–4
  Bruner and Postman (1947) 28–31
  Herlitz et al. (1997) 32
  Jacobs (1887) 20–7
  template 24–7, 78–81

N
natural experiments 17
nominal data 40, 41

O
observed value 40
operationalization of variables 6, 12
opportunity sampling 62
order effects 18, 19
ordinal data 40, 41

P
participant variables 13, 18
pie charts 38, 70
pilot study 61
placebos 6
Postman 28
practical research skills 4, 5
pre-existing characteristics of participants 6, 17
probability 39–40

Q
quasi-experiments 17

R
random sampling 61–2
repeated measures design (RMD) 17, 18–19, 41
repeated t-test 41, 51–3
research methods 12–19
research report
  abstract 64–5
  aims and hypotheses 65–6
  analysis component 68–71
  appendices 72–5
  assessment criteria 8–9
  descriptive results 69–70
  design and methodology 66–8
  discussion 71–2
  evaluation component 71–2
  exploration component 66–8
  inferential results 71
  introduction 65
  introduction component 64–6
  references 72
  title page 64
researcher bias 14

S
sampling 61–2
'screw you' phenomenon 14, 62
self-selected sampling 62
serial digit span 21
sign test 41–2
significance 39–40
single-blind procedure 14
situational variables 13
skills 4–5
social desirability bias 14
standardized instructions 58–9

T
tables 37
transferable skills 4, 5
twins 19
Type I error 39
Type II error 40

V
validity iv
variables 6, 12–13
volunteer sampling 62

W
Wilcoxon signed-matched ranks test 41, 47–8